Vanuatu travel guide 2023

Vanuatu Unveiled: A Journey through Nature, Culture, and Adventure

Spencer Reynolds

WELCOME TO VANUATU 4

WHY VISIT VANUATU? 6

PLANNING YOUR TRIP.........................9

BEST TIME TO VISIT VANUATU 9

TRAVEL ESSENTIALS: VISAS, CURRENCY, AND SAFETY TIPS 12

HEALTH AND SAFETY PRECAUTIONS: 14

CULTURAL SENSITIVITY AND RESPECT: 14

CHOOSING YOUR ACCOMMODATIONS: RESORTS, BUNGALOWS, AND GUESTHOUSES..........................16

EMBRACE NATURE'S BOUNTY 19

EXPLORING VANUATU'S STUNNING BEACHES...........19

ISLAND HOPPING ADVENTURES 22

VANUATU'S MARINE WONDERS: SNORKELING AND DIVING HOTSPOTS......................................27

DISCOVERING THE MAGNIFICENT WATERFALLS AND CAVES..32

EXPERIENCING VANUATU'S CULTURE...36

UNRAVELING THE MELANESIAN HERITAGE 36

FESTIVALS AND CELEBRATIONS 41

KASTOM VILLAGES 45

THRILLS AND ADVENTURES....................51

TREKKING THROUGH VANUATU'S LUSH JUNGLES 51

ZIPLINING AND CANOPY TOURS............................57

ACTIVE VOLCANOES: WITNESSING THE POWER OF NATURE..62

WATERSPORTS GALORE: SURFING, KAYAKING, AND PADDLE BOARDING..68

DELIGHTS OF VANUATU CUISINE 73

A GASTRONOMIC ADVENTURE: TRYING LOCAL
DELICACIES 73
TOP RESTAURANTS AND STREET FOOD GEMS 78
COOKING CLASSES: LEARN TO PREPARE VANUATU'S
TRADITIONAL DISHES 83

CONNECTING WITH THE LOCALS 88

SHOPPING IN VANUATU: LOCAL CRAFTS AND
SOUVENIRS 88
LEARNING THE ART OF WEAVING AND CARVING 94

PRACTICAL TIPS FOR A SEAMLESS
JOURNEY 99

TRANSPORTATION WITHIN VANUATU: TAXIS, BUSES,
AND FERRIES 99
LANGUAGE AND COMMUNICATION 104
HEALTH AND SAFETY GUIDELINES 109

VANUATU ITINERARIES 113

ONE WEEK ITINERARIES 113
WEEKEND ITINERARIES 118

CONCLUSION 122

Welcome to Vanuatu

Did you know that in Vanuatu, you can dive into underwater post offices, hike to mesmerizing lava lakes, and witness fearless locals take the plunge from towering wooden towers? Welcome to a world where natural wonders collide with heart-pounding adventures, and every day promises a new surprise! Come and discover why Vanuatu is the South Pacific's ultimate playground for thrill-seekers and nature enthusiasts alike!

Welcome to the enchanting world of Vanuatu, a hidden gem nestled in the heart of the South Pacific. In "Vanuatu Unveiled: A Journey through Nature,

Culture, and Adventure," we invite you to embark on a voyage like no other, uncovering the wonders of this tropical paradise in 2023.

Vanuatu, an archipelago of over 80 islands, offers a kaleidoscope of experiences waiting to be discovered. From the stunning beaches with powdery sand and crystal-clear waters to the lush jungles teeming with exotic wildlife, each island in Vanuatu promises a unique and awe-inspiring adventure.

Picture a breathtaking tapestry of landscapes, ranging from soaring volcanic peaks to turquoise lagoons and cascading waterfalls. Vanuatu's diverse geography creates an inviting playground for nature enthusiasts and thrill-seekers alike. As you explore this tropical haven, you'll be greeted by a warm and equable climate, offering the perfect setting for year-round adventures and relaxation under the Pacific sun.

The heart of Vanuatu lies in the rich culture and traditions of the Ni-Vanuatu people. With over 110 languages spoken, each community bears its distinct heritage, welcoming visitors with open arms and genuine warmth. In "Vanuatu Unveiled," we offer cultural insights and introduce you to the customs, ceremonies, and way of life that have thrived for generations. Connect with the locals, witness mesmerizing land diving rituals, and become part of a tapestry of traditions that will leave a lasting imprint on your soul.

Step into a world where adventure beckons, where natural beauty mesmerizes, and where the spirit of Vanuatu embraces you with open hearts. "Vanuatu Unveiled: A Journey through Nature, Culture, and Adventure" is your passport to an extraordinary travel experience, blending insider insights, practical tips, and sustainable tourism initiatives.

Are you ready to uncover the secrets of Vanuatu in 2023? Let "Vanuatu Unveiled" be your gateway to a world of wonder, inspiration, and cherished memories. Embrace the allure of this captivating archipelago, where nature's wonders and the warmth of the Ni-Vanuatu people await your arrival. Open the pages of this guide and set forth on an unforgettable journey through Vanuatu's breathtaking landscapes, vibrant culture, and thrilling adventures that will stay with you long after you return home. The paradise of Vanuatu awaits your discovery, and "Vanuatu Unveiled" is your key to unlocking its hidden treasures.

Why visit Vanuatu?
Nestled in the heart of the South Pacific, Vanuatu is a tropical archipelago renowned for its untouched beauty, vibrant culture, and warm hospitality. Often referred to as the "Happiest Place on Earth," this island nation offers a unique and unforgettable experience for travelers seeking an authentic escape

from the bustling world. From breathtaking landscapes to rich cultural heritage, here are compelling reasons why you should consider visiting Vanuatu.

Pristine Natural Beauty:

Vanuatu boasts an unparalleled natural beauty that will leave you in awe. Imagine white sandy beaches fringed by swaying palm trees, crystal-clear turquoise waters teeming with marine life, and lush rainforests home to an astonishing variety of flora and fauna. The archipelago is a haven for adventure enthusiasts, offering opportunities for snorkeling, diving, hiking, and even volcano exploration. Witness the majestic Mount Yasur, one of the most accessible and active volcanoes in the world, providing an enthralling display of lava eruptions against the night sky.

Rich Cultural Heritage:

Steeped in ancient traditions, Vanuatu offers an immersive cultural experience that sets it apart from other destinations. The island's unique Melanesian heritage is still vividly alive in its customs, dances, music, and rituals. Visit local villages to witness traditional ceremonies, interact with friendly locals, and gain insights into their age-old ways of life. One such cultural highlight is the extraordinary Naghol Land Diving ritual, an ancient tradition that inspired modern-day bungee jumping.

Warm Hospitality:

Vanuatu's people are renowned for their genuine warmth and friendliness, making visitors feel like part of the community. Locals often welcome travelers with open arms, sharing their customs and stories, which create lasting memories and enrich your overall experience. This hospitality is especially evident during the many cultural festivals celebrated throughout the year, where you can witness captivating performances and partake in communal feasts.

Serenity and Relaxation:

Escape the stress and monotony of everyday life by indulging in Vanuatu's laid-back ambiance. The tranquil atmosphere and slow-paced lifestyle provide an excellent setting for relaxation and rejuvenation. Bask in the sun on pristine beaches, take a leisurely dip in natural hot springs, or simply unwind with a traditional massage. Vanuatu's serene environment offers the perfect opportunity to unplug and reconnect with nature and yourself.

Mouthwatering Cuisine:

Vanuatu's cuisine is a delightful fusion of fresh produce, seafood, and local flavors. Savor delicious dishes prepared using traditional cooking methods and ingredients. Sample dishes like laplap (a yam-based pudding), coconut crab, and local fish cooked in fragrant coconut milk. Food enthusiasts will be treated to a gastronomic adventure, indulging in tastes that can only be experienced on these unique Pacific islands.

Sustainable Tourism:

Vanuatu takes pride in its commitment to sustainable tourism practices, ensuring the preservation of its natural wonders and cultural heritage for generations to come. By visiting Vanuatu, you contribute to the local economy and help support initiatives that protect the environment and empower the community.

Conclusion:

Vanuatu is a paradise on Earth, offering a blend of untouched natural beauty, rich cultural heritage, and warm hospitality. It is a destination that not only captivates the senses but also nourishes the soul. Whether you seek adventure, relaxation, or a cultural awakening, Vanuatu has something to offer everyone. Embrace the magic of this South Pacific gem and create memories that will last a lifetime. So, pack your bags and embark on a journey to discover the enchanting allure of Vanuatu.

Planning Your Trip

Best Time to Visit Vanuatu

As you step onto the sun-kissed shores of Vanuatu, a world of natural wonders and cultural treasures awaits you. The ideal time to visit this enchanting South Pacific archipelago can greatly influence the experiences you'll encounter. Each season in Vanuatu offers a unique tapestry of delights, from thrilling adventures to captivating cultural festivals. In this narrative, we will delve into the best time to visit Vanuatu, accompanied by insider tips and recommendations to ensure you have an unforgettable and enriching journey.

April to October: A Tropical Oasis in the Dry Season

Imagine yourself sipping on a coconut, reclining under the shade of a palm tree, and gazing at the azure waters stretching before you. From April to October, Vanuatu basks in the embrace of the dry season. The weather is at its most inviting, with comfortable temperatures, minimal rainfall, and gentle sea breezes. This period is perfect for indulging in water activities like snorkeling, diving, and kayaking, as the underwater visibility reaches its peak. Explore the vibrant marine life, swim among colorful coral reefs, and encounter majestic sea turtles gliding gracefully beneath the waves.

- Insider Tip: Venture to the picturesque island of Espiritu Santo during this time. Explore the world-famous Blue Hole, a mesmerizing natural wonder where the clarity of the water invites you to dive into its depths.

November to February: Embrace Festivity and Island Spirit

As the year unfolds, Vanuatu comes alive with joyous festivities and a palpable island spirit. From November to February, the archipelago celebrates its cultural heritage with vibrant festivals, spirited dances, and the warmest hospitality. Embrace the festivities of Christmas and New Year in a tropical paradise, where local communities come together in a symphony of color and rhythm. Engage in customary ceremonies, witness sacred rituals, and participate in traditional feasts that celebrate the essence of Vanuatu's rich Melanesian culture.

- Insider Tip: Make your way to the island of Pentecost in December and January to witness the awe-inspiring land diving ceremony, a ritual of bravery and tradition that involves local men leaping from tall towers with vines tied to their ankles.

March: Embrace the Green Season's Beauty

March marks the transition into Vanuatu's Green Season, a time when the islands are replenished by refreshing tropical rains. While you may encounter occasional showers, the lush landscapes burst into life with an abundance of greenery and blossoming flowers. This season is a paradise for nature enthusiasts and photographers seeking to capture the dramatic beauty of the rainforests and waterfalls in their prime. The temperatures remain pleasant, and the region is less crowded, offering a tranquil escape for those seeking a deeper connection with nature.

- Insider Tip: Wander through the enchanting Mele Cascades on Efate Island during March. The falls are at their most magnificent, and the rejuvenating natural pools provide a serene sanctuary.

Conclusion:

Vanuatu is a destination of year-round allure, and the best time to visit depends on your interests and desires. Whether you seek aquatic adventures amidst crystal-clear waters or wish to immerse yourself in the island's vibrant cultural heritage, Vanuatu has something to offer in every season. With insider tips and recommendations in your arsenal, you are poised to embrace the magic of this tropical oasis fully. So, let the seasons guide your journey, and let the essence of Vanuatu captivate your heart, creating memories that will linger long after you depart its shores.

Travel Essentials: Visas, Currency, and Safety Tips

Embarking on a voyage to the picturesque islands of Vanuatu promises a world of breathtaking beauty and cultural immersion. As you plan your adventure, it's essential to be well-prepared with travel essentials to ensure a smooth and enriching experience. From securing the right visas to managing currency and prioritizing safety, this narrative will guide you through every aspect of your journey to Vanuatu, enriched with insider tips and recommendations for a truly unforgettable expedition.

Visas and Entry Requirements:

Before setting sail to Vanuatu, ensure you have the necessary travel documents and visas in order. Citizens of most countries can obtain a visa on arrival for a stay of up to 30 days. However, it's crucial to check the latest visa regulations on the official Vanuatu government website or consult the nearest embassy or consulate. Ensure your passport is valid for at least six months beyond your intended departure date from Vanuatu.

- Insider Tip: Carry printed copies of your accommodation bookings and return flight details as these may be required for immigration purposes.

Currency and Money Matters:

The currency of Vanuatu is the Vanuatu Vatu (VT), and while some larger establishments accept credit cards, it's advisable to carry cash, especially in more remote areas. ATMs can be found in major towns and cities, but it's best to withdraw enough cash for your trip in advance. Inform your bank of your travel plans to avoid any issues with using your cards overseas.

- Insider Tip: Consider bringing small denominations of the Australian Dollar (AUD), as it is widely accepted in Vanuatu and can serve as a backup currency.

Health and Safety Precautions:
Vanuatu is generally a safe destination, but it's essential to take basic precautions to ensure your well-being during your stay. Stay hydrated in the tropical climate by carrying a refillable water bottle and using sunscreen and protective clothing. While tap water is generally safe to drink in urban areas, it's advisable to opt for bottled water in more remote locations.

- Insider Tip: Pack insect repellent to protect against mosquitoes, especially if you plan to venture into jungle areas or during dusk and dawn.

Cultural Sensitivity and Respect:
Vanuatu's rich cultural heritage is a significant part of its allure, and respecting local customs and

traditions is vital. When visiting villages or participating in ceremonies, seek permission from the community and follow any guidelines provided. Dress modestly when outside of resorts or beaches, and avoid wearing hats in villages, as it is considered disrespectful.

- Insider Tip: Engage in the local "Bislama" language – a pidgin English widely spoken in Vanuatu – as a gesture of goodwill and appreciation for the culture.

Environmental Responsibility:

As a responsible traveler, help preserve the natural beauty of Vanuatu by practicing eco-friendly habits. Avoid littering, especially in marine environments, and participate in organized beach clean-ups when possible. Use reef-safe sunscreen to protect the delicate marine ecosystem during water activities.

Insider Tip: Support local sustainable tourism initiatives and community-based projects that contribute positively to the preservation of Vanuatu's environment and culture.

Conclusion:

A journey to Vanuatu is an opportunity to immerse yourself in a captivating world of tropical wonders and vibrant culture. By being well-prepared with the right visas, currency, and safety precautions, you can embark on a truly unforgettable adventure.

Embrace the spirit of Vanuatu with cultural sensitivity and environmental responsibility, cherishing every moment of your experience. Armed with insider tips and recommendations, let your journey to this idyllic South Pacific paradise leave an indelible mark on your heart, and return home with cherished memories that will last a lifetime.

Choosing Your Accommodations: Resorts, Bungalows, and Guesthouses

In the idyllic paradise of Vanuatu, where turquoise waters meet white sandy beaches and lush rainforests beckon, finding the perfect accommodation is an integral part of your memorable journey. As you plan your stay in this South Pacific gem, you'll encounter a diverse array of options, each offering a unique experience. From luxurious resorts to rustic bungalows and charming guesthouses, this narrative will guide you through the enchanting world of Vanuatu's abodes, accompanied by insider tips and recommendations to ensure your stay is nothing short of extraordinary.

Resorts: Indulge in Luxury Amidst Nature's Embrace

Vanuatu's luxury resorts offer an unparalleled blend of opulence and natural beauty. Picture yourself waking up to the soothing sound of waves crashing on the shore, stepping out onto your private terrace with breathtaking ocean views, and being pampered with world-class amenities. Resorts in Vanuatu often feature stunning infinity pools, exclusive spa facilities, and a range of dining options serving delectable cuisine.

- Insider Tip: For an indulgent experience, opt for an overwater bungalow at one of the upscale resorts. These idyllic accommodations allow you to witness mesmerizing marine life directly from your doorstep.

Bungalows: Embrace Rustic Tranquility in Nature's Lap

For a more authentic and intimate connection with Vanuatu's natural beauty, consider staying in a traditional bungalow. These charming structures are often made from local materials and blend seamlessly with their surroundings. Wake up to the melodious sounds of birds chirping and rustling leaves, as you relish the simplicity and tranquility of island life.

- Insider Tip: Seek out eco-resorts that offer bungalows with sustainable practices, ensuring you have a memorable experience while leaving a minimal environmental footprint.

Guesthouses: Embrace Local Hospitality and Culture

Immerse yourself in Vanuatu's warm hospitality and vibrant culture by choosing to stay in a guesthouse. These family-run accommodations provide a unique opportunity to interact with locals, learn about their customs, and partake in traditional meals. Guesthouses often offer a home-away-from-home ambiance, creating a sense of belonging and authenticity during your stay.

- Insider Tip: Consider staying in a guesthouse on one of the more remote islands for a genuine and off-the-beaten-path experience.

Location: Deciding Between Beachfront and Jungle Retreats

Vanuatu offers an array of accommodation options, each boasting its unique location. Choose a beachfront resort for direct access to the inviting waters, the soothing sounds of the ocean, and stunning sunsets. On the other hand, opt for a jungle retreat to be enveloped by the lush rainforest, listen to the symphony of tropical birds, and revel in the seclusion of nature.

- Insider Tip: If you're torn between the two, consider a split-stay, experiencing both beachfront and jungle retreat accommodations to savor the best of both worlds.

Conclusion:

As you embark on your Vanuatu adventure, the choice of accommodation becomes an integral part of your overall experience. Whether you prefer the lavish comforts of a resort, the rustic charm of a bungalow, or the cultural immersion of a guesthouse, each option promises a distinct journey. From indulgent luxury to authentic connections with nature and locals, Vanuatu's abodes cater to every traveler's desires. Armed with insider tips and recommendations, let the choice of your accommodation be a reflection of your spirit, and let your stay in this tropical oasis leave you with cherished memories to cherish for a lifetime.

Embrace Nature's Bounty

Exploring Vanuatu's Stunning Beaches

Vanuatu, a hidden gem in the South Pacific, is a tapestry of natural wonders, and its beaches stand as glittering jewels in this tropical paradise. From the moment you set foot on the islands, you are welcomed by the enchanting symphony of powder-soft sand beneath your feet, turquoise waters gently caressing the shore, and swaying palm trees painting a serene backdrop against the azure sky. Embark on an unforgettable journey of exploration as we unveil some of Vanuatu's most stunning beaches, each offering its own unique allure and charm.

Champagne Beach, Espiritu Santo Island:

Aptly named for its effervescent beauty, Champagne Beach on Espiritu Santo Island is a vision of heavenly proportions. As you stroll along its seemingly endless stretch of powdery white sand, you'll find yourself mesmerized by the pristine beauty that surrounds you. Crystal-clear, shallow waters gently lap the shore, inviting you to take a refreshing dip and explore the underwater wonders. The beach's magic lies in the underwater volcanic vents that create tiny bubbles, evoking the effervescence of champagne, making your swimming experience nothing short of magical.

Encircled by majestic cliffs that add an air of grandeur to this postcard-perfect scene, Champagne Beach is a true Vanuatu gem.

Hideaway Island, Efate Island:

Escape to the intimate allure of Hideaway Island, nestled just a short boat ride away from Efate Island. True to its name, this beach is a secluded paradise, offering a retreat into the wonders of nature. Embark on an underwater adventure as you snorkel or dive in the coral-fringed waters, where vibrant marine life thrives. Dive deeper and discover the famous underwater post office, where you can send waterproof postcards to your loved ones, creating a memorable connection from this idyllic island hideaway.

Port Olry, Espiritu Santo Island:

For those seeking tranquility away from the crowds, Port Olry on Espiritu Santo Island is a hidden oasis waiting to be discovered. This unspoiled gem captivates visitors with its untouched charm, where coconut trees sway gently, providing natural shade as you indulge in the serenity of the surroundings. The clear waters beckon you for a refreshing swim, offering an escape into blissful solitude. Savor the moment with a beachside picnic, taking in the untouched beauty of this Vanuatu treasure.

Bokissa Beach, Bokissa Private Island:

For a taste of exclusivity and seclusion, Bokissa Private Island awaits with open arms. Embrace the luxurious escape that this pristine beachfront offers, providing the perfect setting to unwind and immerse yourself in unparalleled natural beauty. With limited visitors, you can relish the feeling of having an entire beach to yourself, creating an intimate connection with the serenity of the ocean breeze and the rhythmic lull of the waves. Bokissa Beach promises a sanctuary of relaxation and rejuvenation, making it a truly indulgent experience.

Lonnoc Beach, Espiritu Santo Island:

Prepare to be awe-struck as you set foot on Lonnoc Beach on Espiritu Santo Island. This postcard-perfect destination leaves a lasting impression with its majestic limestone cliffs framing the powdery white sand and inviting waters. During low tide, a series of natural rock pools form, inviting you to explore and wade in their crystal-clear waters. As the sun begins its descent, Lonnoc Beach transforms into a surreal canvas, providing a breathtaking backdrop for the awe-inspiring sunset. It's a sight that will etch itself into your heart forever.

Conclusion:

Vanuatu's stunning beaches are a testament to the natural beauty that lies within this South Pacific paradise. Each beach offers a unique charm and allure, captivating the soul and creating cherished memories. Whether you seek seclusion in the lap of luxury, a hidden oasis away from the world, or a picturesque postcard scene to immerse in nature's embrace, Vanuatu's beaches promise an unforgettable adventure. As you explore the islands' coastline, let the beauty of these stunning beaches leave an indelible mark on your heart, and may your journey in Vanuatu be filled with moments of serenity, wonder, and bliss.

Island Hopping Adventures

Vanuatu's archipelago, with its myriad of islands scattered across the South Pacific, beckons adventurers to embark on a journey of discovery through the art of island hopping. Each island is a treasure trove of natural beauty, rich culture, and unique experiences waiting to be uncovered. Island hopping in Vanuatu promises a kaleidoscope of adventures, from indulging in pristine beaches to delving into ancient traditions and immersing in the warm hospitality of the locals. In this exhilarating narrative, we invite you to join us as we explore the wonders of Vanuatu's archipelago through island hopping adventures.

Efate Island: The Gateway to Vanuatu

Begin your island-hopping odyssey in Efate, the main island and gateway to Vanuatu. The capital city, Port Vila, welcomes you with its vibrant markets, quaint cafes, and bustling waterfront. Take a dip in the pristine waters of Mele Cascades and explore the fascinating underwater world at Hideaway Island's underwater post office. Efate offers an array of water activities, cultural tours, and culinary delights, setting the stage for the adventures that lie ahead.

Espiritu Santo Island: Unspoiled Beauty and Blue Holes

Next, venture to Espiritu Santo, Vanuatu's largest island, and prepare to be captivated by its unspoiled beauty. Explore the famous Champagne Beach, where powdery white sand meets crystalline waters, creating an ethereal paradise. Dive into the mystical allure of the Blue Holes, a network of freshwater swimming spots surrounded by lush jungle, inviting you to cool off in their enchanting waters.

Tanna Island: Mystical Volcanic Experiences

Island hop to Tanna, a land of ancient customs and dramatic volcanic landscapes. Witness the awe-inspiring Mount Yasur, one of the most accessible active volcanoes globally, as it puts on a fiery display against the night sky. Immerse yourself in the island's cultural heritage by visiting traditional villages and partaking in age-old customs, gaining insights into the timeless way of life of the locals.

Pentecost Island: Land Diving Rituals

A visit to Pentecost Island promises an unforgettable encounter with one of Vanuatu's most remarkable traditions – the land diving ritual. Marvel at the bravery and cultural significance of local men as they dive from tall towers with vines tied to their ankles, symbolizing a bountiful yam harvest. This centuries-old ritual is a testament to the island's unique cultural heritage.

Ambrym Island: Mystical Magic and Black Magic

Ambrym Island beckons adventurers seeking to delve deeper into Vanuatu's mystique. Known as the "Black Magic" island, Ambrym is shrouded in intrigue and ancient beliefs. Trek through the otherworldly landscape to the rim of Mount Marum's active volcano, witnessing a mesmerizing lava lake that seems to emerge from the depths of the Earth.

Tongoa Island: Serenity and Cultural Immersion

Continuing your island-hopping adventure, set sail for Tongoa Island, a lesser-known gem that offers a serene escape from the bustle of modern life. Here, time seems to slow down, inviting you to embrace the island's tranquility and immerse yourself in the welcoming embrace of the local communities. Engage in cultural exchanges with the villagers, who are eager to share their traditions, songs, and stories. Participate in weaving sessions, learning the art of crafting traditional mats, hats, and baskets from palm fronds – a skill passed down through generations. As the sun sets, join in the mesmerizing custom of island dancing, where rhythmic beats and swaying movements celebrate the island's vibrant heritage.

Mystery Island: A Secluded Paradise

Venture to Mystery Island, a place that lives up to its enigmatic name. This uninhabited islet lies near Tanna Island and provides a secluded paradise, perfect for relaxation and basking in the natural wonders of Vanuatu. Wander along its pristine shores, discovering hidden coves and secret lagoons. Dive into the crystal-clear waters to explore the vibrant coral reefs, teeming with colorful marine life. The untouched beauty of Mystery Island invites you to unwind and reflect, offering a sense of serenity found only in the most remote corners of the world.

Malekula Island: Enchanting Cultural Diversity

As you continue your island-hopping odyssey, set foot on Malekula Island, a land brimming with captivating cultural diversity. Here, you'll encounter unique traditions, languages, and customs that have flourished for centuries. Immerse yourself in the island's vibrant cultural tapestry, visiting different villages, each with its distinct identity and practices. Witness traditional ceremonies and dances that reflect the deep-rooted spirituality and ancestral beliefs of the local communities. Don't miss the chance to taste the island's diverse cuisine, indulging in traditional dishes made from fresh, locally sourced ingredients.

Ambae Island: A Volcanic Eden

Ambae Island, also known as Aoba, offers a dramatically different landscape from its volcanic counterpart, Ambrym. As you step onto this lush island, you'll be greeted by tropical rainforests, cascading waterfalls, and fertile valleys. Ambae is a haven for nature lovers, providing ample opportunities for trekking and birdwatching amidst the dense foliage. Immerse yourself in the island's pristine wilderness, where the call of exotic birds serenades you as you explore this ecological paradise. For an ethereal experience, visit Lake Manaro, a sacred crater lake formed within the active volcano at the island's center, offering a tranquil setting to reflect on the wonders of nature.

Conclusion:

Vanuatu's archipelago, with its myriad of islands scattered across the South Pacific, presents a paradise for adventurers seeking the art of island hopping. Each island offers a captivating blend of natural beauty, rich culture, and unique experiences, inviting you to explore and uncover their hidden treasures. From the bustling markets and pristine beaches of Efate to the volcanic landscapes and mystical traditions of Tanna and Ambrym, each destination paints a vivid canvas of beauty and cultural heritage. Immerse yourself in the warm hospitality of the locals, savor the taste of traditional cuisine, and witness age-old rituals that have withstood the test of time. As you hop from one enchanting island to another, let the wonders of Vanuatu's archipelago leave an indelible mark on your heart, creating cherished memories that will linger long after you depart these tropical shores.

Vanuatu's Marine Wonders: Snorkeling and Diving Hotspots

Vanuatu's aquatic realm is a mesmerizing underwater playground, where vibrant coral reefs, exotic marine life, and crystal-clear waters beckon snorkelers and divers alike. Tucked away in the heart of the South Pacific, this island nation boasts a treasure trove of marine wonders, providing a kaleidoscope of colors and experiences for all underwater enthusiasts. In this immersive journey, we invite you to dive deep into the marine hotspots of Vanuatu, where each dive and snorkel promises encounters with some of the most stunning underwater vistas on the planet.

SS President Coolidge, Espiritu Santo Island:

Prepare to be awe-struck by the SS President Coolidge, one of the world's most accessible and captivating wreck dives. This former luxury liner turned troopship sank during World War II, and now rests in the tranquil waters off Espiritu Santo

Island. Dive down to explore the remnants of this colossal ship, which is now adorned with colorful coral formations and inhabited by an abundance of marine life. The wreck's vastness allows for multiple dives, revealing different parts of the ship and offering divers a thrilling journey back in time.

Million Dollar Point, Espiritu Santo Island:

Another fascinating dive site off Espiritu Santo Island is Million Dollar Point, an underwater graveyard of military equipment and machinery. After World War II, the American forces dumped a vast collection of equipment into the ocean, creating an extraordinary artificial reef. The site is now home to a diverse array of marine life, including schools of fish, rays, and even occasional visits from reef sharks. Dive among the remnants of history and witness how nature has transformed a once solemn site into a thriving marine ecosystem.

Hideaway Island, Efate Island:

Not only a paradise for snorkelers, but Hideaway Island is also a haven for divers seeking unique experiences. The island's famous underwater post office allows divers to mail waterproof postcards, creating cherished memories that can be treasured long after the journey ends. Snorkelers will also be delighted by the colorful marine life in the shallows, while divers can explore the nearby coral gardens and underwater caves. With easy access from Port

Vila, Hideaway Island is a must-visit destination for water enthusiasts of all levels.

Mele Cascades, Efate Island:

On Efate Island, the Mele Cascades is not just a beautiful waterfall, but also a fantastic snorkeling spot. Take a short hike to the falls and cool off in the refreshing natural pools. While swimming near the falls, keep an eye out for small fish and other aquatic creatures that thrive in these pristine waters. Snorkeling in this unique freshwater setting amidst lush surroundings adds a distinctive touch to your aquatic adventures in Vanuatu.

Tranquility Island Marine Sanctuary, Efate Island:

For snorkelers looking to explore a marine sanctuary, Tranquility Island off Efate's shores is a must-visit spot. This protected area is dedicated to preserving the coral reef and marine life, providing a sanctuary for a diverse range of underwater creatures. Snorkelers can observe vibrant corals, reef fish, and even turtles gliding gracefully through the waters. The calm and clear conditions make it an ideal snorkeling destination for both beginners and experienced enthusiasts.

Recommendations for Snorkelers and Divers Exploring Vanuatu's Marine Wonders:

- Safety First: Before embarking on any snorkeling or diving adventure, ensure you have proper training and certification if required. Follow the guidelines of your tour operator or dive shop and adhere to safety procedures during your underwater excursions.
- Respect the Marine Environment: Be a responsible diver or snorkeler by avoiding touching or disturbing marine life and corals. Remember that you are a visitor in their home, and respecting their habitat helps preserve the delicate marine ecosystem.
- Carry Reef-safe Sunscreen: Choose reef-safe sunscreen to protect both your skin and the marine environment. Traditional sunscreens containing harmful chemicals can harm coral reefs and marine life when washed off into the water.
- Dive with Local Operators: Support local businesses and dive operators in Vanuatu. They have extensive knowledge of the dive sites and marine life, and diving with them enhances your overall experience while contributing to the local economy.
- Stay Hydrated and Practice Good Health Habits: Snorkeling and diving activities can be physically demanding, so make sure to stay hydrated and be aware of any health limitations before participating in underwater activities.

- Capture Memories Respectfully: Bring an underwater camera to capture the beauty of Vanuatu's marine wonders, but do so without disturbing marine life or touching fragile corals. Remember that some marine species, like turtles, are protected, and it's best to observe them from a respectful distance.
- Opt for Eco-friendly Tour Operators: Choose dive and snorkel operators that promote eco-friendly practices, such as responsible waste disposal, conservation initiatives, and education about marine conservation.
- Practice Buoyancy Control: Improving your buoyancy control skills not only enhances your diving experience but also minimizes the risk of accidentally damaging corals or marine life with your equipment.
- Discover Night Diving: If you have the opportunity, try a night dive to witness a whole new world come alive. Many marine creatures are more active at night, and it's a unique experience you won't want to miss.
- Support Marine Conservation Efforts: Consider participating in marine conservation activities, such as reef clean-ups or citizen science initiatives, to actively contribute to the preservation of Vanuatu's marine ecosystem.

Remember, exploring Vanuatu's marine wonders is a privilege, and responsible practices ensure that these underwater treasures continue to thrive for generations to come. Enjoy the magic of the South Pacific's aquatic paradise while leaving only footprints and taking away cherished memories of a once-in-a-lifetime experience.

Conclusion:

Vanuatu's marine wonders provide an underwater paradise for snorkelers and divers seeking unforgettable experiences. From exploring historic shipwrecks and artificial reefs to encountering a vibrant array of marine life in crystal-clear waters, each diving and snorkeling hotspot in Vanuatu offers a unique and captivating adventure. Whether you're a seasoned diver or a novice snorkeler, the underwater vistas of Vanuatu promise to leave you breathless and filled with wonder. As you immerse yourself in the aquatic wonders of this South Pacific gem, let the vibrant coral reefs, exotic marine life, and the magic of Vanuatu's underwater world create lasting memories that will stay with you long after you return to the surface.

Discovering the Magnificent Waterfalls and Caves

Nestled in the heart of the South Pacific, Vanuatu is a tropical paradise renowned for its pristine beaches, lush rainforests, and vibrant marine life. Beyond the sun-kissed shores, the island nation hides a treasure trove of natural wonders, including awe-inspiring waterfalls and mystical caves waiting to be explored. Embark on an unforgettable journey as we delve into the magnificent world of Vanuatu's waterfalls and caves, each offering a unique and breathtaking experience.

Mele Cascades: A Refreshing Oasis on Efate Island

Located just a short drive from the capital city of Port Vila on Efate Island, Mele Cascades is a refreshing oasis that delights visitors with its cascading beauty. As you embark on a scenic hike through the lush rainforest, the sound of rushing water guides you towards the falls. Marvel at the series of crystal-clear pools formed by the cascading waters, inviting you to cool off and unwind in nature's embrace. The main waterfall, standing at an impressive height, offers an exhilarating plunge pool at its base, creating a perfect spot for a revitalizing dip. This tranquil setting amidst verdant greenery provides a peaceful escape from the world, leaving you feeling rejuvenated and invigorated.

Rarru Cascades: A Hidden Gem on Pentecost Island

Venture off the beaten path to Pentecost Island, where the hidden gem of Rarru Cascades awaits. This lesser-known waterfall presents a secluded oasis, accessible only through a scenic trek through the island's wilderness. As you approach the falls, the pristine waters gushing over the rocks become a mesmerizing sight. The natural pools beneath the cascades offer a serene setting for relaxation and reflection. Swim in the cool waters, surrounded by the untouched beauty of Pentecost's rainforest, and let the peaceful atmosphere wash over you.

Lope Lope Lodge Caves: Mystical Underground Wonders on Espiritu Santo Island

Step into the mystical world of Lope Lope Lodge Caves on Espiritu Santo Island, where subterranean wonders await. These limestone caves present a fascinating underground landscape, adorned with stalactites and stalagmites, which have formed over millennia. Guided tours lead you through dimly lit passages, where you'll discover impressive chambers and breathtaking rock formations. Learn about the cultural significance of these caves to the local Ni-Vanuatu people and marvel at the ancient markings on the cave walls. The cool, damp air inside the caves creates an otherworldly ambiance, making it a surreal and unforgettable experience.

Millennium Cave: A Thrilling Adventure on Espiritu Santo Island

For those seeking an adrenaline-pumping adventure, the Millennium Cave on Espiritu Santo Island is a must-visit destination. Accessible through a challenging hike and river trek, the cave offers a once-in-a-lifetime experience. Explore its vast chambers, traversing along underground streams and cascading waterfalls. The cave's name is derived from the fact that it was first explored in the year 2000, and since then, it has become a popular destination for intrepid explorers. The journey to the Millennium Cave takes you through dense rainforest, crossing bamboo bridges, and even includes a thrilling zipline ride across the river. This immersive experience into the heart of Vanuatu's wilderness is an unforgettable adventure for adventurers of all ages.

Blue Cave: A Magical Marine Grotto on Tanna Island

Tanna Island, known for its majestic volcano, also harbors a marine wonder known as the Blue Cave. Accessible only by boat, this enchanting grotto is concealed beneath limestone cliffs, which creates a natural play of light and water, giving the cave its ethereal blue hue. As you glide into the cave on a small boat, you'll be mesmerized by the interplay of sunlight and the crystal-clear waters, illuminating the cave in mesmerizing shades of blue. Snorkelers can explore the cave's underwater wonders, where schools of fish and vibrant coral formations thrive. The Blue Cave's tranquil and surreal atmosphere creates a sense of serenity and wonder, making it a truly magical experience.

Conclusion:

Vanuatu's magnificent waterfalls and caves offer a glimpse into the island nation's natural wonders, transporting visitors to a world of beauty and mystery. From the refreshing oasis of Mele Cascades on Efate Island to the mystical underground landscape of Lope Lope Lodge Caves on Espiritu Santo Island, each destination presents a unique and unforgettable experience. Whether you seek relaxation amidst cascading waters or thrill in exploring hidden subterranean realms, Vanuatu's waterfalls and caves promise an immersive journey into the heart of nature's enchantment. As you uncover these natural treasures, allow yourself to be captivated by the beauty and magic of Vanuatu's lesser-known wonders, leaving you with cherished memories of a truly extraordinary adventure in the South Pacific.

Experiencing Vanuatu's Culture

Unraveling the Melanesian Heritage

Nestled in the embrace of the South Pacific, the archipelago of Vanuatu holds a rich and diverse cultural tapestry known as Melanesia. Melanesian heritage is an intricate web of traditions, customs, and beliefs that have flourished across the islands for thousands of years. Steeped in ancestral wisdom, these traditions are an integral part of daily life, connecting the present to the past and offering a window into the unique identity of the Ni-Vanuatu people. In this immersive journey, we delve into the heart of Melanesian heritage, unveiling the cherished customs and traditions that shape the vibrant culture of Vanuatu.

The Vanuatu People: Warm Hospitality and Community Spirit

One of the defining characteristics of Melanesian heritage is the warm hospitality and strong community spirit exhibited by the Vanuatu people. Visitors to the islands are greeted with open arms, as locals are eager to share their customs and traditions with those who seek to understand their way of life. The sense of community and belonging is deeply rooted in Melanesian culture, as families and villages work together in harmony to preserve their heritage and pass down knowledge from one generation to the next.

Kastom: The Living Tradition of Vanuatu

At the heart of Melanesian heritage lies the concept of "Kastom," a living tradition that governs the customs, beliefs, and social structures of the Ni-Vanuatu people. Kastom is not just a set of rituals or practices but an intricate worldview that encompasses all aspects of life, from birth to death. It encompasses various elements such as kinship systems, land ownership, and ceremonies that mark significant life events. Each island and village has its distinct Kastom, reflecting the diversity and uniqueness of Vanuatu's cultural landscape.

Nakamal: The Center of Community Life

In every village across Vanuatu, you will find a Nakamal, a traditional meeting place and social hub. The Nakamal is a sacred space where the men of the community gather to discuss matters of importance, share stories, and make decisions that impact their village. It is also a place for spiritual rituals, such as kava ceremonies, which hold great significance in Melanesian heritage. The Nakamal plays a vital role in maintaining the strong sense of community and fostering a deep connection to the land and ancestral roots.

Sand Drawing: Preserving History Through Art

An art form unique to Vanuatu, sand drawing serves as a visual representation of the island's history and cultural heritage. Elders and storytellers use the sand to create intricate patterns and symbols, each carrying a specific meaning that recounts the tales of their ancestors. Sand drawing is a captivating way to preserve history, as these ephemeral artworks are created during ceremonies and rituals, connecting the present generation to the wisdom of the past.

Custom Dances and Celebrations: Vibrant Expression of Identity

Custom dances and celebrations are an exuberant display of Vanuatu's cultural identity, and each island showcases its distinct dance forms and rhythms. These performances often take place during festivals, gatherings, or special occasions, where the vibrancy of the costumes and the rhythmic beats of traditional instruments captivate onlookers. Through dance, stories are told, legends are brought to life, and the essence of Melanesian heritage is shared with pride and joy.

Respect for Ancestors and Nature: Harmony with the Universe

In Melanesian heritage, a profound respect for ancestors and nature is woven into the fabric of daily life. Ancestral spirits are believed to guide and protect the living, and their wisdom is sought in times of decision-making and important ceremonies. A deep connection to the land and natural environment is evident in the way resources are used sustainably and in the rituals that pay homage to the elements and spirits that inhabit the islands.

Ceremonies and Rituals: Milestones of Life

Throughout Vanuatu, ceremonies and rituals mark significant milestones in life, such as birth, coming-of-age, marriage, and death. These rituals are imbued with spiritual significance and are conducted with great reverence and precision. The ceremonies often involve the entire community, strengthening the bonds between generations and reinforcing the collective identity of the village or tribe.

Conclusion:

Unraveling the Melanesian heritage of Vanuatu offers a profound journey into a world of rich traditions, customs, and beliefs that have endured the test of time. From the warm hospitality and community spirit of the Vanuatu people to the living tradition of Kastom that shapes their way of life, each aspect of Melanesian heritage holds a significant place in the hearts of the Ni-Vanuatu. The Nakamal, sand drawing, custom dances, and ceremonies all contribute to the vibrant expression of their cultural identity. With a deep respect for ancestors and nature, the Ni-Vanuatu maintain a harmonious relationship with the universe, fostering a profound connection to the land and the spirits that inhabit it.

As visitors immerse themselves in the rich tapestry of Melanesian heritage, they are welcomed into a world of storytelling, celebration, and ancient wisdom. The customs and traditions of Vanuatu provide an invaluable glimpse into the resilience and spirit of a people who honor their past while embracing the future. By preserving and sharing their cultural heritage, the Ni-Vanuatu ensure that their identity remains alive, vibrant, and cherished for generations to come.

Festivals and Celebrations

Vanuatu, the jewel of the South Pacific, is not only a land of breathtaking natural beauty but also a place where celebrations and festivals hold a special place in the hearts of its people. The vibrant culture of Vanuatu comes alive during these joyous occasions, which showcase the island nation's rich traditions, customs, and community spirit. Joining in the festivities offers visitors a unique opportunity to immerse themselves in the warm embrace of Vanuatu's cultural heritage. In this immersive journey, we will unravel the magic of Vanuatu's festivals and celebrations, offering insider insights into the heart of these joyous events.

Vanuatu Independence Day: Celebrating Unity and Freedom

Vanuatu Independence Day, celebrated on July 30th, is one of the most significant events in the country's calendar. This day commemorates the nation's independence from colonial rule and is marked by colorful parades, cultural performances, and vibrant festivities throughout the islands. The air is filled with excitement and national pride as locals and visitors alike come together to celebrate the unity and freedom of the nation. Traditional dances, music, and feasts are held to honor the diverse cultures that make up Vanuatu's population, fostering a sense of shared identity and pride in their heritage.

Nagol (Land Diving): A Spectacular Rite of Passage

Nagol, also known as land diving, is an ancient rite of passage practiced on Pentecost Island. This centuries-old tradition, famously known as the precursor to modern bungee jumping, is an awe-inspiring spectacle that attracts visitors from around the world. Taking place during the yam harvest season, brave men leap from wooden towers with vines tied to their ankles, symbolizing a successful harvest and fertility. The ritual is believed to ensure a bountiful yam crop and is accompanied by dances, chants, and blessings from the village elders. Witnessing Nagol is a humbling experience, as the courage and cultural significance behind this ancient custom leave a lasting impression on all who are fortunate enough to be part of it.

Vanuatu Fest Napuan: A Melodic Fusion of Cultures

Vanuatu Fest Napuan is a music festival that showcases the country's diverse musical talent and cultural heritage. Held annually in Port Vila, this vibrant event brings together musicians, dancers, and artists from across the islands for a week of lively performances and musical collaborations. Traditional string bands, contemporary musicians, and cultural dance groups grace the stages, offering a fusion of Melanesian beats and modern tunes. The festival creates a harmonious space where locals and visitors can come together to celebrate the power of music and its ability to unite people across cultures.

Back to My Roots Festival: Embracing Indigenous Heritage

The Back to My Roots Festival is a celebration of Vanuatu's indigenous heritage and is held on the island of Tanna. This unique festival invites people from different tribes and islands to reconnect with their ancestral roots, sharing stories, dances, and rituals that have been passed down through generations. The event aims to preserve and celebrate traditional customs while fostering a sense of belonging and pride in one's cultural heritage. It is a time of reflection and gratitude, as the younger generation learns from their elders, ensuring that these ancient traditions remain alive and cherished.

Toka Festival: Honoring Ancestral Spirits

Toka Festival is a sacred event celebrated on Ambrym Island, known for its mystical beliefs and customs. During this festival, the Ni-Vanuatu people come together to honor their ancestors and ancestral spirits. The festival is marked by traditional dances, ceremonies, and rituals that seek blessings and protection from the spirits. Toka is not merely a religious event but a cultural phenomenon that binds the community together, fostering a strong sense of unity and reverence for their ancestors.

Rom Dance: Ritual of Love and Courtship

Rom Dance, also known as Rom Dancing, is a captivating courtship ritual practiced on Malekula Island. During this enchanting dance, young men and women express their feelings of love and attraction through graceful movements and rhythmic steps. The dance is a vital part of the courtship process and allows the participants to showcase their elegance and charm while seeking potential partners. Rom Dance not only celebrates the beauty of courtship but also reinforces the sense of community and connection among the island's youth.

Conclusion:

Festivals and celebrations are a window into the soul of Vanuatu's vibrant culture, offering an opportunity to experience the island nation's rich traditions, customs, and community spirit firsthand.

From the exuberance of Vanuatu Independence Day to the awe-inspiring land diving ritual of Nagol, each festival reflects the unique identity and pride of the Ni-Vanuatu people. The musical fusion of Vanuatu Fest Napuan, the embrace of indigenous heritage in the Back to My Roots Festival, the spiritual reverence of Toka Festival, and the enchanting courtship ritual of Rom Dance all come together to create a tapestry of cultural celebration that leaves a lasting impact on all who take part.

Participating in these joyous occasions allows visitors to become a part of the warm and welcoming Vanuatu community, forging connections that go beyond the beauty of the islands' landscapes. As travelers join in the celebrations, they are enveloped in the spirit of unity, pride, and reverence for ancestral wisdom that forms the very essence of Melanesian heritage. Vanuatu's festivals and celebrations are a testament to the power of culture, music, dance, and rituals in preserving and passing down the cherished traditions of a nation that celebrates life with unmatched exuberance and joy.

Kastom Villages
In the enchanting archipelago of Vanuatu, the true essence of Melanesian heritage comes alive in the Kastom Villages. These unique communities are living museums that offer an immersive journey into the heart of Vanuatu's cultural traditions, customs, and way of life. Nestled amidst lush

tropical landscapes, Kastom Villages provide an opportunity for visitors to step back in time and experience the rich tapestry of indigenous wisdom that has been passed down through generations. In this in-depth exploration, we unveil the magic of Kastom Villages, sharing insider insights into the profound cultural significance and warm hospitality that awaits those who venture to these hidden gems.

Kastom: The Soul of Vanuatu's Cultural Heritage

To understand Kastom Villages, one must first grasp the concept of "Kastom," a unique and all-encompassing worldview that governs the lives of the Ni-Vanuatu people. Kastom is a living tradition that reflects the beliefs, customs, and social structures of each village, ensuring the preservation of ancestral knowledge and wisdom. It serves as a guiding force that defines the unique identity of each community, establishing a deep connection to the land, the spirits, and the ancestors.

In Kastom Villages, Kastom is not just an abstract idea but an integral part of daily life. Every aspect of existence, from birth to death, is governed by Kastom customs and rituals, providing a sense of continuity and harmony with the natural world. The elders of the village are the keepers of this sacred knowledge, passing it down to the younger generations through storytelling, dances, ceremonies, and practical skills.

The Architecture of Kastom Villages: Living in Harmony with Nature

The architecture of Kastom Villages embodies the essence of harmony with nature. Traditional dwellings, known as "nakamals" or "nisnas," are crafted using locally sourced materials, such as bamboo, thatch, and pandanus leaves. These traditional structures are designed to withstand the elements while allowing for natural ventilation and connection to the environment.

The layout of Kastom Villages often centers around a communal open space, where daily activities, ceremonies, and gatherings take place. This central area serves as the heart of the village, fostering a sense of unity and community spirit. Surrounding the central space, individual family compounds are nestled, each with its small garden and space for private activities. The village's spatial organization reflects the deep-rooted respect for community life and the significance of living in harmony with both the human and natural world.

Village Leadership and Governance: The Wisdom of Elders

Kastom Villages operate on a system of traditional governance, with elders playing a central role in decision-making and maintaining social order. The village chief, known as the "big man" or "nakamal man," holds significant authority and is revered for their wisdom, leadership, and connection to ancestral spirits. Decisions are made through consensus, with elders' guidance and community involvement ensuring the well-being and harmony of the village.

The wisdom of the elders extends beyond governance, as they are the repositories of traditional knowledge, oral histories, and cultural practices. They are the custodians of the village's sacred sites, ensuring the preservation of spiritual and cultural heritage. The passing down of this wisdom to younger generations is fundamental to the continuity and resilience of Kastom Villages.

Ceremonies and Rituals: Connecting with Ancestral Spirits

Ceremonies and rituals are integral components of life in Kastom Villages, marking significant events and connecting the living with ancestral spirits. These spiritual practices are deeply rooted in the belief that the spirits of ancestors play a vital role in guiding and protecting the community.

Among the many ceremonies, the most profound and revered is the Nakamal, a traditional gathering in the village's central meeting space. Nakamals are held to seek guidance from ancestral spirits, resolve conflicts, celebrate cultural milestones, and offer gratitude for the harvest. The ceremonies are accompanied by traditional dances, chants, and offerings, creating a spiritual and deeply emotive experience that leaves an indelible mark on participants.

Village Crafts and Traditional Skills: Ancient Artistry

Kastom Villages are also centers of craftsmanship and traditional skills, where artisans create exquisite handcrafted items that showcase the island's cultural artistry. From intricate wood carvings to woven mats, baskets, and handicrafts, each piece reflects the cultural heritage and artistic expression of the village's people.

These skills are passed down through generations, with elders mentoring young apprentices in the traditional techniques. The process of crafting these items is not only a means of economic sustenance but also a deeply spiritual practice that connects the artisan with their ancestors and the spirits of the land.

Sharing in the Spirit of Kava: A Symbol of Unity

Central to the social fabric of Kastom Villages is the ceremonial drink known as kava. Made from the roots of the kava plant, this mild intoxicant is consumed during special gatherings and ceremonies as a symbol of unity and shared community spirit.

The kava ceremony is a revered tradition, with specific rituals and protocols followed during its preparation and consumption. The communal act of partaking in kava fosters a sense of bonding, mutual respect, and camaraderie among the village members and visitors alike. It is a gesture of hospitality, as sharing kava represents an invitation to join in the customs and traditions of the Kastom Village.

Experiencing Kastom Villages: Embracing the Warm Hospitality

Visiting a Kastom Village offers an authentic and transformative cultural experience. As a visitor, it is essential to approach the village with respect, openness, and a willingness to learn and appreciate the nuances of Kastom.

When visiting a Kastom Village, it is customary to seek permission from the village chief and elders. A village guide or local liaison can serve as a bridge between visitors and the community, facilitating understanding and ensuring cultural sensitivity.

Participating in village activities, ceremonies, and crafts can further enrich the experience, fostering a deep connection with the local culture and its people. Embracing the warm hospitality of the Kastom Villages allows visitors to become a part of the community, forging connections that go beyond the boundaries of time and place.

Conclusion:

Kastom Villages are the soul of Vanuatu's cultural heritage, embodying the wisdom, traditions, and customs of the Ni-Vanuatu people. These living museums offer an immersive journey into the heart of Melanesian culture, providing visitors with an authentic glimpse of a way of life deeply rooted in harmony with nature and spiritual reverence for ancestors.

In Kastom Villages, the ancient and the contemporary seamlessly merge, as the wisdom of the elders guides the younger generations in preserving and passing down their cultural heritage. From the architecture of the village to the governance by the elders, every aspect reflects the interconnectedness of the village's people with the land, spirits, and ancestral wisdom.

Visiting a Kastom Village is not just a glimpse into the past but an opportunity to connect with a living culture that continues to thrive amidst the changing world. Embracing the warm hospitality and sharing in the spirit of community allows visitors to become part of a larger tapestry, where the wisdom of Kastom offers valuable insights into the enduring human connection to nature, ancestors, and one another. In the hidden gems of Kastom Villages, the true magic of Vanuatu's cultural heritage comes to life, leaving a lasting impression on all who embark on this profound journey of discovery.

Thrills and Adventures

Trekking Through Vanuatu's Lush Jungles

Nestled in the heart of the South Pacific, Vanuatu is a tropical paradise renowned for its breathtaking landscapes, pristine beaches, and vibrant marine life. Beyond the sun-kissed shores, the island nation hides a lush and mysterious world, waiting to be explored—the dense jungles of Vanuatu. Embarking on a trek through these emerald realms offers adventurers an opportunity to connect with nature's bounty, witness unique flora and fauna, and experience the warm embrace of the island's wilderness. In this immersive exploration, we unveil the magic of trekking through Vanuatu's lush jungles, offering insider insights into the awe-inspiring beauty and untamed allure of the island's natural wonders.

The Hidden Gems of Espiritu Santo: Millennium Cave and Mount Tabwemasana

The island of Espiritu Santo boasts some of Vanuatu's most stunning jungle treks, leading explorers to hidden gems of unparalleled beauty. One such gem is the Millennium Cave, a thrilling adventure that takes trekkers deep into the heart of the jungle. The journey to the cave involves hiking through dense rainforest, crossing rivers, and even soaring across canyons on a zipline. Upon reaching the cave, a mesmerizing underground world awaits, with crystal-clear pools, waterfalls, and stunning limestone formations.

For more experienced trekkers, conquering Mount Tabwemasana, Vanuatu's highest peak, offers an exhilarating challenge. The ascent through the dense jungle leads to rewarding panoramic views of the island and the opportunity to experience the untouched wilderness of Espiritu Santo from a different perspective.

Tanna Island: Trekking to the Fiery Heart of Yasur Volcano

Tanna Island is known for its mystical landscapes, and the trek to Mount Yasur provides a once-in-a-lifetime adventure. Mount Yasur is one of the world's most accessible active volcanoes, and trekking to its fiery heart is an awe-inspiring experience. As night falls, the volcano lights up the sky with its fiery display, offering trekkers a surreal and unforgettable sight.

The journey to Mount Yasur takes trekkers through diverse terrain, from lush rainforests to barren volcanic landscapes. Along the way, visitors can encounter the island's unique flora and fauna, including endemic bird species and vibrant tropical plants. The experience of standing at the rim of the volcano, feeling the rumbling of the earth beneath, is a humbling reminder of the raw power and beauty of nature.

Efate Island: Mele Cascades and Summiting Mount Vila

On Efate Island, the capital city of Port Vila serves as the gateway to various trekking opportunities. The Mele Cascades, located just a short drive from the city, offer an enchanting jungle trek that leads to a series of stunning waterfalls and natural pools. The lush vegetation and the sound of rushing water create a serene and rejuvenating atmosphere, making it an ideal spot to escape into nature's embrace.

For trekkers seeking a more challenging endeavor, summiting Mount Vila offers panoramic views of Port Vila and the surrounding coastline. The trek starts with a journey through lush jungles, gradually ascending to higher elevations. As trekkers climb higher, they are rewarded with breathtaking views and a sense of accomplishment as they conquer the peak.

Ambrym Island: The Mystical Journey to Mount Marum

Ambrym Island beckons adventurers seeking a truly mystical jungle trek to the rim of Mount Marum. This active volcano boasts one of the largest lava lakes in the world, and the trek to its crater offers an otherworldly experience. The journey through Ambrym's dense jungles takes trekkers to the volcanic highlands, where the rugged landscape and ethereal beauty create an unforgettable sense of adventure.

Upon reaching the crater's edge, trekkers are met with a breathtaking sight—a mesmerizing lava lake, seemingly emerging from the depths of the Earth. The sight and sound of the bubbling lava create a sense of wonder and reverence for the power of nature. The experience of standing at the rim of an active volcano is an adventure like no other, leaving trekkers with a profound appreciation for the earth's untamed forces.

Pentecost Island: Exploring Enchanting Waterfalls and Highlands

Pentecost Island's lush jungles hold treasures waiting to be discovered. Exploring the island's waterfalls, such as the Rarru Cascades, offers a refreshing and tranquil escape. The trek to Rarru Cascades takes trekkers through dense forests, crossing streams, and navigating through rocky terrain. The reward is a pristine and secluded waterfall, surrounded by the untouched beauty of Pentecost's wilderness.

For a more immersive journey, trekking through the highlands of Pentecost Island offers a chance to witness the island's rural way of life and encounter traditional villages. The island's rugged landscape and fertile valleys create an enchanting backdrop for exploration, offering trekkers a glimpse into the traditions and customs that have endured for generations.

Insider Tips for Jungle Trekking in Vanuatu

Trekking through Vanuatu's lush jungles is an exhilarating adventure, but it requires careful preparation and awareness of the natural environment. Here are some insider tips for an unforgettable trekking experience:

- Local Guides: Engage the services of local guides who are familiar with the terrain and cultural aspects of the region. They can provide valuable insights into the flora, fauna, and cultural significance of the areas you traverse.
- Respect Nature: As you venture through the jungles, respect the environment and wildlife. Avoid leaving behind any traces of your visit and refrain from disturbing the natural habitats of the island's creatures.
- Weather and Terrain: Be prepared for varying weather conditions and terrains. Wear appropriate clothing and footwear that can withstand the challenges of the jungle. Carry essential items such as insect repellent, sunscreen, and sufficient water for hydration.
- Cultural Sensitivity: When visiting villages during your treks, practice cultural sensitivity by seeking permission before taking photographs or participating in ceremonies.

Respect local customs and traditions, and show appreciation for the warm hospitality of the island's people.

Conclusion:

Trekking through Vanuatu's lush jungles is a journey into nature's embrace, offering adventurers a chance to connect with the untamed beauty and mystery of the island's wilderness. From hidden gems on Espiritu Santo to the fiery heart of Yasur Volcano on Tanna, the jungles of Vanuatu unfold a tapestry of awe-inspiring experiences.

The island's diverse terrains, rich flora, and unique fauna create an immersive environment for exploration, while encounters with the island's cultural heritage add depth and meaning to the trekking experience. As trekkers navigate through dense rainforests, ascend volcanic peaks, and discover enchanting waterfalls, they become part of the rhythm of nature, leaving behind a sense of wonder and reverence for the earth's natural wonders.

The magic of trekking through Vanuatu's lush jungles lies not only in the physical challenges but also in the spiritual connection to the land, its people, and the wisdom of nature itself. This immersive journey offers a transformative experience that lingers in the heart long after the trek is complete, beckoning adventurers to return to nature's embrace time and time again.

Ziplining and Canopy Tours

Vanuatu, the tropical paradise in the South Pacific, is not only renowned for its pristine beaches and vibrant marine life but also for its lush jungles teeming with natural wonders. Beyond the idyllic coastlines lies a verdant world waiting to be explored—the dense canopies of Vanuatu's jungles. For adventure seekers and nature enthusiasts, trekking through these emerald realms and experiencing the thrill of ziplining and canopy tours offers an unforgettable adventure in nature's playground. In this immersive exploration, we unveil the magic of trekking through Vanuatu's lush jungles and taking to the skies on exhilarating ziplining and canopy tours, providing insider insights into the breathtaking beauty and heart-pounding excitement of these unique experiences.

The Natural Playground of Tanna Island

Tanna Island, known for its dramatic landscapes and mystical allure, offers a thrilling jungle trek that culminates in a captivating ziplining experience. The trek takes adventurers through dense rainforests, where towering trees and exotic flora create an enchanting backdrop. The lush foliage is home to a myriad of bird species and unique wildlife, offering trekkers the chance to encounter some of Vanuatu's endemic creatures along the way.

As the trek reaches its pinnacle, participants are treated to a heart-pounding adventure—the exhilarating zipline. Suspended high above the jungle floor, the zipline allows adventurers to glide through the canopies with breathtaking views of the surrounding landscapes. The rush of adrenaline and the feeling of soaring above the treetops provide a sense of freedom and connection with nature that is truly unparalleled.

Espiritu Santo: Adventure and Serenity in the Jungles

Espiritu Santo, Vanuatu's largest island, is a haven for nature lovers and adrenaline enthusiasts alike. Trekking through the island's lush jungles offers a chance to witness the unspoiled beauty of the region. The dense foliage creates a cool and serene atmosphere, making it an ideal escape from the tropical heat.

For those seeking a unique adventure, combining trekking with ziplining is an excellent option. Ziplining tours on Espiritu Santo take participants through the canopies, offering bird's-eye views of the pristine landscapes and hidden waterfalls below. The zipline's thrilling descent provides an adrenaline rush, while the tranquil surroundings create a sense of calm and serenity—a perfect balance of excitement and relaxation.

Efate Island: An Aerial Adventure Above the Rainforest

Efate Island, home to the capital city of Port Vila, offers a different perspective on jungle trekking with its thrilling canopy tours. These tours take participants high above the rainforest, where suspension bridges and platforms allow for a bird's-eye view of the lush landscapes below.

The canopy tours are not only an exciting adventure but also an educational experience. Knowledgeable guides offer insights into the rich biodiversity of Vanuatu's rainforests, pointing out unique plant species and explaining their ecological importance. The tours also highlight the conservation efforts in place to preserve these precious ecosystems for future generations.

Safety and Sustainability: The Key to Enjoying Canopy Tours

Safety is of paramount importance in canopy tours, and operators in Vanuatu prioritize the well-being of participants. High-quality equipment, trained guides, and strict safety protocols ensure that adventurers can enjoy their experience with peace of mind.

Additionally, sustainability is a fundamental aspect of canopy tours in Vanuatu. Operators strive to minimize their environmental impact, following eco-friendly practices that preserve the natural beauty of the rainforests and support local conservation initiatives. By participating in canopy tours, visitors contribute to the protection of

Vanuatu's natural heritage, allowing future generations to enjoy these pristine environments.

Insider Tips for a Memorable Trekking and Ziplining Experience

- Dress Appropriately: Wear comfortable and breathable clothing suitable for trekking and ziplining. Closed-toe shoes with good grip are essential for traversing uneven terrain and participating in ziplining activities.
- Stay Hydrated: Carry sufficient water to stay hydrated throughout the trek and ziplining experience. The tropical climate can be dehydrating, so it's crucial to drink plenty of fluids.
- Pack Essentials: Bring sunscreen, insect repellent, and a hat to protect yourself from the sun and insects while trekking through the jungles.
- Listen to the Guides: Pay attention to the guides' instructions during the trek and ziplining tour. They are knowledgeable about the area and will ensure your safety and enjoyment during the adventure.
- Embrace the Moment: Take time to soak in the natural beauty of Vanuatu's jungles and appreciate the exhilaration of ziplining through the canopies. Be present in the moment and savor the unique experience.

Conclusion:

Trekking through Vanuatu's lush jungles and experiencing the thrill of ziplining and canopy tours offers a rare opportunity to connect with nature's playground in the South Pacific. From Tanna Island's mystical landscapes to Espiritu Santo's unspoiled beauty and Efate Island's aerial adventure, each experience provides a unique perspective on the island's natural wonders.

As adventurers trek through dense rainforests, encounter endemic wildlife, and glide through the canopies on ziplines, they become immersed in the magic of Vanuatu's untamed wilderness. The thrill of ziplining is balanced with the serenity of the jungle, creating an unforgettable harmony between excitement and tranquility.

Moreover, responsible operators prioritize safety and sustainability, ensuring that participants can enjoy their experience while preserving the natural beauty of the rainforests for generations to come. Trekking through Vanuatu's lush jungles and embarking on ziplining and canopy tours is an adventure of a lifetime, where the heart races with adrenaline, and the soul finds solace in nature's embrace.

Active Volcanoes: Witnessing the Power of Nature

In the heart of the South Pacific lies an enchanting archipelago known as Vanuatu—a land of stunning landscapes, pristine beaches, and vibrant marine life. But amidst its tropical beauty, there lies a dramatic awe-inspiring phenomenon that captivates adventurers and nature enthusiasts alike—the presence of active volcanoes. Vanuatu is home to several active volcanoes, offering a rare and unforgettable opportunity to witness the raw power of nature at work. In this immersive exploration, we delve into the world of active volcanoes in Vanuatu, providing insider insights into the geological wonders, the cultural significance, and the sheer thrill of witnessing the earth's primal forces in action.

The Ring of Fire: Vanuatu's Volcanic Legacy

Vanuatu, situated along the Pacific Ring of Fire, is part of a vast and volatile region characterized by active tectonic plate boundaries and numerous volcanic arcs. The Ring of Fire is notorious for its seismic activity, including earthquakes and volcanic eruptions. In Vanuatu, this geological phenomenon has shaped the island's landscapes, giving rise to magnificent volcanic structures that dominate the horizon.

The tectonic forces that converge in the region create a unique and dynamic environment, making Vanuatu a geological paradise for scientists and a fascinating destination for adventure-seekers.

Tanna Island: The Fiery Heart of Yasur Volcano

Tanna Island, one of Vanuatu's most mystical and culturally rich islands, is home to one of the world's most accessible active volcanoes—Mount Yasur. Known locally as the "Fiery Mountain," Mount Yasur is a sacred and revered site for the Ni-Vanuatu people, who believe it to be the home of their ancestral spirits.

Trekking to the rim of Mount Yasur offers an exhilarating adventure through diverse terrain, from lush rainforests to barren volcanic landscapes. As night falls, the real spectacle begins—the fiery show of the volcano's lava eruptions. Standing at the edge of the crater, visitors witness the rhythmic explosions and spewing of molten lava into the night sky—a sight that evokes both wonder and trepidation.

The experience of witnessing Mount Yasur's eruptions is a humbling reminder of the earth's immense power and the delicate balance between creation and destruction.

Ambrym Island: The Black Magic and Mysticism of Mount Marum

Ambrym Island is another volcanic gem in Vanuatu, known for its unique cultural practices and the mystical allure of Mount Marum. Often referred to as the "Black Magic Island," Ambrym is steeped in tradition, and the volcano holds immense spiritual significance for the local communities.

The trek to Mount Marum is an arduous journey through dense jungles and rugged volcanic landscapes. As trekkers ascend to the rim of the active volcano, they are rewarded with a breathtaking sight—the mesmerizing lava lake, seemingly emerging from the depths of the Earth. The sight and sound of the bubbling lava create an otherworldly experience, leaving an indelible mark on those who dare to venture to this volcanic heart.

The cultural and spiritual significance of Mount Marum adds a layer of mystique and enchantment to the already extraordinary adventure.

Pentecost Island: The Land Diving Tradition

Pentecost Island is renowned for its unique and daring land diving tradition, also known as "Naghol." This ancient ritual involves local men leaping from tall wooden towers with vines tied to their ankles—a practice believed to ensure a bountiful yam harvest.

The ritual is performed during the yam harvest season, attracting visitors from around the world to witness this extraordinary display of courage and cultural heritage. The practice is not without risks, and land divers rely on their skill and faith in the traditions passed down through generations.

The land diving tradition is a testament to the resilience and courage of the Ni-Vanuatu people and offers an insight into their deep connection with the land and the forces of nature.

Gaua Island: The Mystical Beauty of Mount Garet

Gaua Island, situated in the northern part of Vanuatu, is home to another of the country's active volcanoes—Mount Garet. Trekking to the summit of Mount Garet offers a challenging yet rewarding adventure, where trekkers can witness the volcanic landscape and explore the crater lake, known as Lake Letas.

The hike to Mount Garet takes adventurers through dense rainforests and across rugged terrains, providing glimpses of the island's untouched beauty along the way. Upon reaching the summit, trekkers are treated to breathtaking views of the surrounding landscape and the majestic crater lake below.

Insider Tips for Witnessing Active Volcanoes in Vanuatu

- Safety First: When witnessing active volcanoes, safety should always be a top priority. Visitors should follow the advice of local guides and authorities, respecting safety zones and adhering to all guidelines.
- Nighttime Spectacles: Some volcanoes, like Mount Yasur, offer the most captivating eruptions during the night. Consider timing

your visit to experience the fiery displays against the backdrop of the dark sky.
- Cultural Respect: When visiting areas with cultural significance, such as Mount Marum on Ambrym Island or land diving ceremonies on Pentecost Island, show cultural respect and seek permission from the local communities.
- Guided Tours: Engaging the services of experienced local guides not only ensures safety but also provides valuable insights into the geological and cultural significance of the volcanic sites.
- Dress Appropriately: Volcanic terrains can be rugged and challenging. Wear sturdy and comfortable footwear, and bring suitable clothing to protect against the elements.

Conclusion:

Witnessing the power of nature in the form of active volcanoes is a thrilling and humbling experience. Vanuatu's volcanic landscapes offer a rare opportunity to connect with the earth's primal forces, leaving visitors in awe of the raw and untamed beauty of the natural world.

From the fiery eruptions of Mount Yasur on Tanna Island to the mystical allure of Mount Marum on Ambrym Island, each volcanic adventure in Vanuatu is a testament to the geological wonders that shape our planet. Moreover, the cultural significance of these volcanic sites adds a layer of depth and enchantment to the experience, providing a glimpse into the deep-rooted beliefs and traditions of the Ni-Vanuatu people.

As adventurers trek through dense jungles, across rugged terrains, and to the rims of active volcanoes, they become witnesses to the earth's constant evolution and the delicate balance between creation and destruction. The experience of witnessing active volcanoes in Vanuatu is a reminder of the planet's infinite beauty, power, and resilience—a transformative encounter with nature's grandeur that lingers in the heart long after the journey is complete.

Watersports Galore: Surfing, Kayaking, and Paddle boarding

Vanuatu, the jewel of the South Pacific, offers much more than just stunning beaches and lush jungles. For watersport enthusiasts and adventure seekers, this tropical paradise is a playground of aquatic delights. With its crystal-clear waters, vibrant marine life, and consistent waves, Vanuatu provides the perfect setting for a wide array of watersports. In this comprehensive guide, we delve into the world of watersports galore in Vanuatu, offering insider insights into the top spots for surfing, kayaking, and paddleboarding, as well as tips for an unforgettable aquatic adventure.

Surfing in Vanuatu: Riding the Waves of Paradise

Surfing in Vanuatu is a well-kept secret among surf enthusiasts, but the island nation's consistent swells and uncrowded breaks make it a dream destination for wave riders. The main surfing hub is on the island of Efate, where the capital city, Port Vila, serves as a gateway to some of the best surf spots in the region.

Pango Point, just a short drive from Port Vila, offers reef breaks that cater to surfers of all levels. The picturesque location, with lush jungles as a backdrop, creates an idyllic setting for catching waves. Nearby breaks such as Breakas and Mele Bay also offer thrilling surf opportunities for those seeking an adrenaline rush.

For more experienced surfers, exploring the surf breaks on Tanna Island, particularly at Sulphur Bay and Lenakel, provides a unique and off-the-beaten-path surfing experience. The stunning landscapes and cultural richness of Tanna add a touch of adventure to the surfing journey.

Kayaking: Paddling Through Vanuatu's Tropical Waters

Kayaking in Vanuatu is a fantastic way to explore the tranquil waters, hidden coves, and pristine coastline of the islands. Whether you're an experienced paddler or a novice, the calm and inviting waters of the South Pacific provide a perfect playground for kayaking adventures.

One of the most popular kayaking destinations is Havannah Harbour on Efate Island. The harbor's sheltered waters and stunning views make it an ideal spot for leisurely paddling or exploring nearby islets. As you glide through the clear waters, keep an eye out for colorful marine life beneath your kayak.

If you seek a more adventurous kayaking experience, consider paddling through the mangroves of Moso Island or exploring the Riri River on Espiritu Santo Island. These waterways offer a chance to witness the rich biodiversity of Vanuatu's coastal ecosystems up close.

Stand-Up Paddle boarding (SUP): Serenity on the Water

Stand-up paddle boarding, or SUP, has become increasingly popular worldwide, and Vanuatu's serene waters provide an excellent playground for this tranquil watersport. SUP offers a unique way to explore the coastline, lagoons, and hidden spots that are often inaccessible by other means.

On Efate Island, Mele Bay is a fantastic location for SUP enthusiasts, with its calm waters and stunning scenery. Paddling along the coastline allows for peaceful moments of connection with nature, as you observe the marine life below and take in the picturesque landscapes.

For those seeking a more adventurous paddle boarding experience, venture to the Blue Lagoon on

Efate Island. This natural wonder boasts crystal-clear waters and a submerged cave perfect for exploring on a SUP. The ethereal blue hues of the lagoon create a magical ambiance, making it a highlight of any paddle boarding adventure in Vanuatu.

Watersports Tips and Safety

- Local Knowledge: Engage the services of local guides or watersports operators who know the best spots for surfing, kayaking, and paddle boarding. Their knowledge of the tides, currents, and local conditions is invaluable for a safe and enjoyable experience.
- Safety Gear: Always wear appropriate safety gear, such as life jackets, especially when paddling in open waters or unfamiliar locations.
- Environmental Conservation: Respect the marine environment and wildlife during your watersports activities. Avoid touching or disturbing marine creatures, and follow responsible snorkeling and diving practices.
- Weather Awareness: Stay informed about weather conditions before embarking on any watersports adventure. Avoid paddling or surfing in dangerous weather or stormy conditions.
- Cultural Sensitivity: When exploring remote or culturally significant areas, show respect for local customs and traditions. Seek

permission before paddling in traditional fishing areas or near local communities.

Combining Watersports and Eco-Tourism

Many watersports operators in Vanuatu are committed to eco-tourism and sustainable practices. Consider supporting businesses that prioritize environmental conservation and actively contribute to the protection of Vanuatu's marine ecosystems.

Participating in beach clean-ups and conservation initiatives organized by local organizations is a rewarding way to give back to the community and help preserve the beauty of Vanuatu's waters for future generations.

Conclusion:

Vanuatu's pristine waters and diverse coastline offer an array of watersports adventures for enthusiasts of all levels. From surfing the waves of paradise to kayaking along tranquil shores and paddleboarding through the crystal-clear waters, the aquatic delights of Vanuatu promise unforgettable experiences.

Surfing in Efate and Tanna, kayaking in Havannah Harbour, and stand-up paddleboarding at Mele Bay and the Blue Lagoon are just a few of the remarkable watersport opportunities awaiting in this tropical paradise.

As you immerse yourself in the wonders of Vanuatu's waters, take a moment to appreciate the fragile beauty of the marine environment. By embracing eco-tourism and sustainable practices, visitors can ensure that the magic of Vanuatu's watersports will continue to thrive for generations to come. Whether you're seeking exhilaration in the surf or serenity on the water, Vanuatu's watersports galore await, ready to create memories that will last a lifetime.

Delights of Vanuatu Cuisine

A Gastronomic Adventure: Trying Local Delicacies

In the heart of the South Pacific lies Vanuatu, a tropical paradise known for its stunning landscapes, pristine beaches, and vibrant culture. But beyond its breathtaking beauty, Vanuatu also offers a mouthwatering culinary scene that reflects the rich diversity of its people and their traditions. For food enthusiasts and adventurous eaters, embarking on a gastronomic adventure in Vanuatu promises an unforgettable journey of the taste buds. From traditional dishes steeped in centuries-old customs to contemporary fusion creations, Vanuatu's local delicacies offer a unique and tantalizing experience. In this comprehensive guide, we will delve into the flavors, aromas, and cultural significance of Vanuatu's culinary delights, providing insider insights into the must-try dishes, unique dining experiences, and the art of savoring the essence of this tropical culinary wonderland.

The Melting Pot of Vanuatu Cuisine:

At the heart of Vanuatu's gastronomy lies a fusion of flavors influenced by its diverse history and cultural heritage. Indigenous traditions blend with the influences of European colonizers and Asian traders, creating a culinary melting pot that celebrates the best of both worlds.

Taro and yams, which are abundant in Vanuatu, form the foundation of many dishes. The root vegetables are traditionally cooked in earth ovens, imparting a unique earthy flavor to the food. Locally caught fish, such as tuna and mahi-mahi, are staples of the island's cuisine, highlighting the importance of the ocean in the lives of the Ni-Vanuatu people.

Must-Try Local Delicacies:

- Lap Lap: A traditional dish that epitomizes the spirit of communal eating in Vanuatu is lap lap. Grated yams or taro are mixed with coconut milk, island cabbage, and sometimes meat or fish. The mixture is then wrapped in banana leaves and cooked in an earth oven, resulting in a flavorful and hearty meal.
- Kokoda: For seafood lovers, kokoda is a must-try delicacy. Similar to ceviche, kokoda features raw fish marinated in lime juice, mixed with coconut milk, and seasoned with chili, onion, and other herbs and spices. The combination of fresh fish and tangy flavors creates a refreshing and delectable treat.
- Nambawan Pies: When it comes to street food, nambawan pies are a popular choice. These savory pastries are filled with a variety of fillings, including minced meat, vegetables, or seafood. Served piping hot, they are a

delicious on-the-go snack enjoyed by locals and visitors alike.

- Tuluk: For a taste of traditional Vanuatu sweets, try tuluk. These bite-sized treats are made from mashed bananas, grated coconut, and sugar, wrapped in banana leaves and cooked in an earth oven. The result is a delightful combination of sweetness and coconutty goodness.

Farm-to-Table Experiences:

In Vanuatu, the concept of farm-to-table is not a trend; it is a way of life. Much of the food consumed on the islands is locally grown and sourced, emphasizing the importance of sustainability and self-sufficiency.

Visiting organic gardens and orchards on Tanna Island or Espiritu Santo offers a unique farm-to-table experience. Guests can explore lush gardens and taste freshly harvested fruits and vegetables, connecting with the agricultural practices that sustain local communities.

The Kava Culture:

A visit to Vanuatu would be incomplete without experiencing the Kava culture, a significant part of the country's social fabric and traditional customs. Kava, made from the roots of the Piper methysticum plant, is served during ceremonial events, meetings, and gatherings.

Participating in a kava ceremony is a unique opportunity to immerse oneself in the local culture. Visitors are welcomed to sit in a circle with locals, and the chief, or "nakamal," serves the kava in a coconut shell. The act of drinking kava is a symbol of friendship and respect, creating lasting connections with the island's culture.

Unique Dining Experiences:

In addition to traditional dishes, Vanuatu offers unique dining experiences that celebrate the island's natural beauty and cultural heritage.

- Beachfront Dining: Many resorts and restaurants in Vanuatu offer beachfront dining, allowing guests to enjoy exquisite meals with their toes in the sand and the soothing sound of the ocean in the background. The combination of delectable cuisine and a stunning backdrop creates a dining experience like no other.
- Fire Dances and Feasts: For a taste of traditional entertainment and cuisine, attend a fire dance performance accompanied by a sumptuous feast. Fire dances are an integral part of Vanuatu's cultural heritage, and the feast that follows showcases a variety of local delicacies.
- Food Festivals: Throughout the year, Vanuatu hosts various food festivals that celebrate local cuisine and showcase the talents of the

island's chefs and farmers. These festivals offer a chance to savor an array of dishes and interact with local producers.

Insider Tips for a Gastronomic Adventure:

- Embrace Local Customs: When dining at local eateries or participating in traditional ceremonies, embrace local customs and show respect for cultural traditions.
- Try New Flavors: Be open to trying new flavors and combinations, as Vanuatu's culinary scene offers a diverse range of dishes.
- Ask the Locals: Locals are a valuable resource for food recommendations and dining tips. Don't hesitate to ask for their suggestions on where to find the best local delicacies.
- Savor the Moment: Take the time to savor each dish and appreciate the effort and love that goes into preparing the food.
- Support Sustainable Practices: Choose restaurants and eateries that prioritize sustainability and support local farmers and producers.

Conclusion:

A gastronomic adventure in Vanuatu is a feast for the senses and an opportunity to connect with the heart and soul of the island's culture. From traditional delicacies like lap lap and kokoda to farm-to-table experiences and the unique kava culture, Vanuatu's culinary scene offers a delightful array of flavors and experiences.

By embracing the richness of Vanuatu's gastronomy, travelers can create lasting memories of the warmth and hospitality of the Ni-Vanuatu people. So, set forth on a culinary journey through the tropical wonderland of Vanuatu, where every bite is a celebration of tradition, community, and the shared joy of savoring the essence of this paradise on a plate.

Top Restaurants and Street Food Gems

Vanuatu, the jewel of the South Pacific, is not only renowned for its breathtaking natural beauty but also for its rich and diverse culinary scene. From traditional dishes rooted in ancient customs to contemporary fusion creations, Vanuatu's gastronomy offers a tantalizing experience for food enthusiasts and adventurous eaters alike. In this comprehensive guide, we explore the top restaurants and street food gems in Vanuatu, offering insider insights into the must-visit dining establishments, local delicacies, and the art of savoring the unique flavors of this tropical paradise.

Tamanu on the Beach: A Culinary Oasis in Efate

Nestled along the shores of Efate Island, Tamanu on the Beach is a culinary oasis that offers an exquisite dining experience. Surrounded by lush gardens and with stunning views of the ocean, the restaurant sets the stage for an unforgettable meal.

Tamanu on the Beach focuses on fresh, locally sourced ingredients, incorporating traditional flavors and contemporary techniques to create a diverse menu. Diners can indulge in dishes like coconut poached lobster, organic garden salads, and mouthwatering desserts crafted with tropical fruits.

For a truly immersive experience, opt for a private beachfront dining setup, where the sound of waves lapping against the shore adds to the ambiance of a perfect evening.

L'Houstalet Restaurant: French-Inspired Delights in Port Vila

For those seeking a taste of France in the heart of Port Vila, L'Houstalet Restaurant is a culinary gem not to be missed. With a charming and romantic setting, this restaurant pays homage to French cuisine while incorporating local ingredients to create an enticing menu.

L'Houstalet offers an array of dishes that showcase the flavors of both France and Vanuatu. From escargots with garlic butter and confit duck to fresh seafood bouillabaisse, each dish is a delightful journey of the taste buds.

The wine selection complements the dining experience, with a variety of French and New World wines to choose from, ensuring that every meal is paired perfectly.

The Waterfront Bar & Grill: Casual Elegance in Port Vila

Perched along the Port Vila waterfront, The Waterfront Bar & Grill exudes casual elegance, making it a favorite dining spot for both locals and visitors. The restaurant's open-air design allows diners to enjoy the sea breeze while taking in stunning views of the harbor.

The menu at The Waterfront features an impressive selection of fresh seafood, including lobster, prawns, and locally caught fish. Steaks and succulent meats are also on offer for those craving heartier fare.

The restaurant's lively atmosphere and live entertainment on select evenings make it an ideal spot for an enjoyable night out.

Chill Restaurant & Bar: A Fusion of Flavors in Port Vila

Located at the award-winning Chantilly's on the Bay resort, Chill Restaurant & Bar offers a fusion of international and Pacific Rim flavors. The restaurant's chic and modern ambiance provides an inviting setting for an elegant dining experience.

Chill's menu boasts an eclectic mix of dishes, from pan-seared scallops and duck breast to Asian-inspired stir-fries and sashimi platters. For dessert, don't miss their delectable tropical fruit pavlova.

With its extensive cocktail menu and a selection of fine wines, Chill is also a great spot for enjoying pre-dinner drinks or a nightcap under the stars.

Street Food Gems: Tasting Vanuatu's Local Flavors

For a more authentic taste of Vanuatu's culinary scene, venture into the vibrant street food scene, where the flavors of the islands come to life.

- Port Vila Markets: The bustling Port Vila Markets are a treasure trove of local delicacies and fresh produce. Here, you'll find nambawan pies, lap lap, and kokoda, as well as tropical fruits like mangoes, papayas, and passion fruit.
- Pango Point Seafood Stalls: Located near Pango Village, the seafood stalls offer a variety of freshly caught fish and seafood cooked to perfection. Try the grilled fish with coconut rice and enjoy the flavors of the sea in a relaxed setting.
- Lamenais Fresh Food Market: This market in Luganville, on Santo Island, is a fantastic place to sample local dishes and interact with friendly vendors. Don't miss out on the chance to try tuluk, a traditional Vanuatu sweet made from mashed bananas and coconut.

Insider Tips for Dining in Vanuatu:

- Reservations: For popular restaurants, especially during peak tourist seasons, it's advisable to make reservations in advance to secure your spot.
- Opening Hours: Some restaurants and street food vendors have limited opening hours, particularly in more remote areas. Be mindful of the opening and closing times to avoid disappointment.
- Cash or Card: While larger restaurants and resorts often accept credit cards, smaller street food vendors and markets may only accept cash. It's a good idea to carry some local currency for convenience.
- Cultural Sensitivity: When dining in local restaurants or markets, show respect for customs and traditions. Some cultural practices, such as drinking kava, may require specific protocols.
- Adventurous Eating: Don't be afraid to try new dishes and flavors. The culinary scene in Vanuatu offers a wide range of tastes and textures to explore.

Conclusion:

A gastronomic adventure in Vanuatu is a journey of flavors and cultural immersion. From fine dining establishments like Tamanu on the Beach and L'Houstalet to the vibrant street food scene, each culinary experience in Vanuatu is a celebration of tradition, community, and the shared joy of savoring the essence of this tropical paradise on a plate.

By exploring the top restaurants and street food gems, travelers can connect with the heart and soul of Vanuatu's culture and people. So, set forth on a culinary exploration of Vanuatu, where every bite is a delightful fusion of history, culture, and the natural bounty of the islands. With a diverse array of flavors waiting to be savored, Vanuatu promises to be a paradise for food enthusiasts and a journey of epicurean delights.

Cooking Classes: Learn to Prepare Vanuatu's Traditional Dishes

Vanuatu, the enchanting jewel of the South Pacific, not only captivates visitors with its breathtaking landscapes but also with its rich culinary heritage. The flavors of Vanuatu's traditional dishes are deeply rooted in its vibrant culture, and what better way to immerse yourself in the island's gastronomy than through cooking classes? Participating in a cooking class in Vanuatu is a unique opportunity to learn the art of preparing authentic dishes, discover the secrets of local ingredients, and gain insight into the cultural significance of food in the lives of the Ni-Vanuatu people. In this comprehensive guide, we will explore the top cooking classes in Vanuatu, offering insider insights into the experiences, the traditional recipes you'll learn, and the unforgettable memories you'll create during this culinary adventure.

Tanna Farms: A Farm-to-Table Experience

Tucked away on the picturesque Tanna Island, Tanna Farms offers a farm-to-table cooking experience like no other. The journey begins with a visit to the farm, where you'll discover the abundant tropical fruits, organic vegetables, and aromatic herbs that form the essence of Vanuatu's cuisine.

Under the guidance of experienced local cooks, you'll learn to prepare traditional dishes such as lap lap and tuluk using fresh ingredients harvested directly from the farm. The hands-on experience of grating yams or taro, mixing coconut milk, and wrapping the mixture in banana leaves is a lesson in authentic island cooking.

As the dishes are cooking in the earth oven, take a moment to appreciate the simplicity and sustainability of traditional Ni-Vanuatu cooking methods. The reward for your efforts will be a delectable meal showcasing the flavors of the island, savored amidst the natural beauty of Tanna.

Le Lagon Resort: A Fusion of Flavors

For travelers staying in Port Vila, the capital city of Vanuatu, Le Lagon Resort offers an enriching cooking class that blends traditional recipes with contemporary flair. The class takes place in a charming outdoor setting, overlooking the resort's lush gardens and shimmering lagoon.

Under the guidance of talented chefs, you'll have the opportunity to learn the art of preparing dishes like kokoda, nambawan pies, and other local delicacies. The chefs at Le Lagon skillfully incorporate modern culinary techniques and presentation styles while staying true to the authentic flavors of Vanuatu.

The class includes a visit to the resort's herb garden, where you'll discover the aromatic spices and herbs used in traditional Ni-Vanuatu cooking. The class culminates in a delightful feast, where you'll enjoy the fruits of your labor in the company of fellow participants.

Jungle Kitchen: A Cultural and Culinary Immersion

Nestled in the lush jungles of Efate Island, Jungle Kitchen offers a truly immersive cooking experience that combines cultural insights with culinary delights. The class begins with a visit to a local market, where you'll learn to select the freshest ingredients for your cooking adventure.

At Jungle Kitchen, you'll have the opportunity to cook alongside local women, who will share their time-honored cooking techniques and family recipes. From traditional lap lap to coconut-infused desserts, each dish is a reflection of the deep connection between food and culture in Vanuatu.

During the class, you'll also learn about the cultural significance of food in local ceremonies and celebrations. The warmth and hospitality of the Ni-Vanuatu people will leave a lasting impression as you bond over a shared love for cooking and food.

Inyeug Island Cooking: A Secluded Culinary Retreat

For a more intimate and secluded cooking experience, Inyeug Island Cooking on Moso Island is the perfect destination. This hidden gem offers a one-of-a-kind opportunity to learn traditional cooking techniques from local experts in a tranquil island setting.

The class starts with a visit to a nearby village, where you'll gain insights into the traditional way of life on Moso Island. You'll gather fresh ingredients from the village gardens and participate in the time-honored process of preparing a meal for the community.

Under the guidance of local cooks, you'll learn to prepare dishes like tuluk and coconut crab, traditional to the island's culture. The cooking process involves using traditional utensils and methods, giving you a true taste of authentic Ni-Vanuatu cooking.

<u>Insider Tips for Enjoying Cooking Classes in Vanuatu</u>:

- Book in Advance: Cooking classes can fill up quickly, especially during peak tourist seasons. It's advisable to book your spot in advance to secure your participation.
- Ask Questions: Don't be afraid to ask questions and interact with the local instructors during the class. They are often eager to share their knowledge and culinary tips with participants.
- Come Hungry: Be prepared to enjoy a hearty meal at the end of the class. Most cooking classes conclude with a feast, where you can savor the dishes you've prepared.
- Respect Local Customs: When visiting local markets or villages as part of the cooking class experience, show respect for cultural customs and traditions.
- Bring an Apron: Some cooking classes may provide aprons, but it's always a good idea to bring one to protect your clothing during the hands-on cooking experience.

Conclusion:

A cooking class in Vanuatu is not merely a lesson in culinary techniques; it is a journey of cultural immersion and discovery. Through hands-on experiences and the guidance of local instructors, you'll gain insight into the heart and soul of Ni-Vanuatu cuisine.

By learning to prepare traditional dishes and understanding the cultural significance of food, you'll create lasting memories of your time in Vanuatu. Whether on a lush farm, by the glistening lagoon, or in the heart of a traditional village, each cooking class offers a unique and unforgettable experience.

So, embark on a culinary adventure in Vanuatu, and let the flavors of the islands awaken your senses and ignite your passion for authentic Ni-Vanuatu cooking.

Connecting with the Locals

Shopping in Vanuatu: Local Crafts and Souvenirs

Vanuatu, the mesmerizing archipelago in the South Pacific, is a treasure trove of natural wonders and vibrant cultural heritage. Beyond its breathtaking landscapes and warm hospitality, Vanuatu offers a vibrant shopping scene that allows visitors to take a piece of this tropical paradise home with them. From intricate handcrafted souvenirs to traditional artifacts and unique creations, shopping in Vanuatu is a delightful experience that reflects the artistry and traditions of the Ni-Vanuatu people. In this comprehensive guide, we explore the top shopping destinations in Vanuatu, revealing the insider insights into the best local crafts, souvenirs, and the cherished memories they bring to life.

Port Vila Handicraft Market: A Shopper's Paradise

Located in the heart of Port Vila, the capital city of Vanuatu, the Handicraft Market is a bustling bazaar that captures the essence of the island's crafts and culture. This vibrant market is a treasure trove of unique and authentic handicrafts, offering an extensive selection of souvenirs and gifts to suit all tastes.

Wander through the maze of stalls to find intricately woven baskets, traditional mats, wood carvings, and colorful sarongs. Handmade jewelry, adorned with shells and local beads, is also a popular find among visitors. Each piece reflects the skill and creativity of the Ni-Vanuatu artisans, making it a meaningful keepsake of your time on the islands.

- Insider Tip: Bargaining is a common practice at the Handicraft Market, so don't hesitate to negotiate the prices to get the best deal on your chosen souvenirs.

Mama's Handicrafts: Empowering Local Women

For a unique and meaningful shopping experience, head to Mama's Handicrafts, a cooperative run by local women on Efate Island. This vibrant boutique showcases a wide range of handmade crafts, all crafted with love and care by the talented women of Vanuatu.

From woven hats and bags to natural beauty products and intricate jewelry, Mama's Handicrafts offers a diverse array of authentic souvenirs. The items here often bear the personal touch of the artisans, making them even more special for travelers looking for one-of-a-kind pieces.

- Insider Tip: Mama's Handicrafts is a socially responsible business that supports local communities. By purchasing from this cooperative, you contribute to empowering and uplifting women in Vanuatu.

Tanna Coffee Factory: Savoring Island's Finest Coffee

For coffee connoisseurs and those seeking unique edible souvenirs, a visit to the Tanna Coffee Factory is a must. Located on Tanna Island, this boutique coffee producer is renowned for producing some of the finest organic coffee in the South Pacific.

The Tanna Coffee Factory offers a variety of coffee blends, from rich dark roasts to milder medium roasts, all sourced from local coffee plantations. The coffee beans are handpicked and sun-dried, ensuring a superior and authentic flavor.

- Insider Tip: Take a guided tour of the Tanna Coffee Factory to learn about the coffee production process, and purchase a bag or two of freshly roasted coffee to bring home.

Market Days in Luganville: A Cultural Experience

In the town of Luganville on Espiritu Santo Island, the local market days are a vibrant celebration of culture and commerce. Held on specific days of the week, the market comes alive with the lively chatter of traders and the aromas of freshly prepared foods.

The market offers an array of locally grown produce, tropical fruits, and traditional foods such as lap lap and coconut-based dishes. Aside from the edible delights, visitors can also find woven crafts, handmade jewelry, and intricate wood carvings.

- Insider Tip: Market days in Luganville are a cultural spectacle. Engage with the friendly locals, taste the traditional cuisine, and soak in the vibrant atmosphere for an authentic experience.

Nakamal at the Beach: Traditional Kava Ceremonies

For a unique souvenir with cultural significance, consider participating in a traditional kava ceremony and taking home your own custom-made kava bowl. Nakamal at the Beach, a popular kava bar in Port Vila, offers this exclusive experience to visitors.

During the ceremony, you'll learn about the preparation and cultural significance of kava, the traditional drink made from the roots of the Piper methysticum plant. After savoring the drink and the camaraderie of the locals, you'll be gifted a kava bowl made by skilled artisans, beautifully adorned with carvings and intricate designs.

- Insider Tip: Kava bowls are prized possessions in Vanuatu and make for a unique and authentic souvenir to commemorate your kava ceremony experience.

Insider Tips for Shopping in Vanuatu:

- Quality Over Quantity: Look for handcrafted items that reflect the artistry and traditions of the Ni-Vanuatu people. Investing in a few high-quality souvenirs will create cherished memories for years to come.
- Sustainable Souvenirs: Choose souvenirs made from sustainable materials, such as woven crafts from pandanus leaves or items made from recycled materials, to support eco-friendly practices.
- Cultural Sensitivity: When purchasing artifacts or souvenirs with cultural significance, be mindful of the cultural customs and traditions associated with them.
- Shipping Options: If you plan to buy larger items or delicate crafts, inquire about shipping options to ensure your purchases arrive safely back home.
- Cash vs. Card: While larger shops and boutiques in tourist areas may accept credit cards, it's advisable to carry some cash, especially when shopping at local markets and smaller businesses.

Conclusion:

Shopping in Vanuatu is a journey of cultural discovery and a celebration of the island's vibrant heritage. From bustling markets to boutique shops and traditional ceremonies, each shopping experience offers a unique insight into the artistry, traditions, and warmth of the Ni-Vanuatu people.

By bringing home authentic handicrafts, locally made souvenirs, and cherished memories, you'll carry a piece of Vanuatu's enchanting spirit with you, long after your visit to this tropical paradise. So, immerse yourself in the vibrant shopping scene of Vanuatu and savor the joy of uncovering treasures that celebrate the essence of this extraordinary island nation.

Learning the Art of Weaving and Carving

Vanuatu, the idyllic archipelago in the South Pacific, is not only renowned for its stunning landscapes and warm hospitality but also for its vibrant cultural heritage. At the heart of this rich culture lies the art of weaving and carving, two ancient crafts that have been passed down through generations. For travelers seeking a deeper connection with the island's traditions, learning the art of weaving and carving is an immersive and rewarding experience. In this comprehensive guide, we delve into the world of these ancient crafts in Vanuatu, offering insider insights into the techniques, cultural significance, and the invaluable knowledge shared by skilled artisans.

The Significance of Weaving and Carving in Vanuatu:

Weaving and carving have been integral to the daily lives of the Ni-Vanuatu people for centuries. These traditional crafts not only produce practical items for daily use but also hold deep cultural and spiritual significance. Both crafts are rooted in local customs, stories, and ceremonies, making them an essential part of Vanuatu's cultural heritage.

Weaving, often done with pandanus leaves, is used to create baskets, mats, hats, and even clothing. These woven items serve as symbols of status, used in traditional ceremonies and events. They also hold practical uses, such as food storage and shelter.

On the other hand, carving is an art form that involves transforming wood and other materials into intricate sculptures, masks, and tools. These carvings often depict mythical creatures, ancestral spirits, and cultural symbols, and they are used in ceremonies, rituals, and storytelling.

Learning Weaving: The Art of Pandanus Weaving

One of the most iconic forms of weaving in Vanuatu is pandanus weaving, which uses the leaves of the pandanus plant. Joining a weaving workshop allows participants to learn the intricate techniques from skilled local weavers and gain insights into the cultural significance of this ancient craft.

During the workshop, you'll learn how to harvest pandanus leaves and prepare them for weaving. The weaving process involves various techniques, including plaiting, coiling, and twining, each producing unique patterns and designs. Experienced weavers will guide you through the steps of creating baskets, hats, and mats, explaining the symbolism behind the patterns and shapes.

- Insider Tip: Weaving workshops are often organized by local communities and cooperatives. Participating in these workshops not only supports the artisans but also provides an authentic cultural exchange.

Carving Workshops: From Wood to Art

Carving is another art form deeply embedded in Vanuatu's culture. The intricate wooden carvings reflect the island's myths, legends, and spiritual beliefs. Participating in a carving workshop is a chance to work with seasoned carvers who possess a wealth of knowledge and skills.

In the workshop, you'll be introduced to the various tools used in carving, such as adzes, chisels, and knives. The instructors will teach you the techniques of shaping the wood, carving intricate patterns, and adding finishing touches to create stunning sculptures and masks.

- Insider Tip: Carving workshops often take place in local villages, offering participants the opportunity to learn in an authentic setting and interact with the local community.

Embracing the Cultural Exchange:

Participating in weaving and carving workshops is more than just a lesson in crafts; it is a gateway to understanding the heart and soul of Vanuatu's culture. As you learn the techniques, you'll also hear the stories and legends associated with the patterns and designs.

The cultural exchange that takes place during these workshops is a profound experience. The artisans will share their knowledge, wisdom, and personal experiences, giving you a deeper appreciation for the art forms and the cultural heritage they represent.

- Insider Tip: Take the time to ask questions and engage in conversations with the artisans. This will not only enhance your learning experience but also create lasting connections and memories.

Supporting Local Artisans and Communities:

When you participate in weaving and carving workshops, you directly contribute to the preservation of these ancient crafts and the livelihood of local artisans. By purchasing their handcrafted creations, you support sustainable tourism and help keep these traditional art forms alive for future generations.

- Insider Tip: Consider purchasing handcrafted woven and carved items directly from local artisans or cooperatives rather than from mass-produced tourist shops. This ensures that your purchase has a direct positive impact on the community.

Weaving and Carving Festivals:

To immerse yourself even further in the world of weaving and carving, try to time your visit to coincide with one of Vanuatu's weaving or carving festivals. These festivals celebrate the artistry of local craftspeople and provide an opportunity to see masterpieces on display, witness traditional performances, and engage with skilled artisans.

- Insider Tip: Keep an eye on local events calendars or ask locals about upcoming festivals and cultural events related to weaving and carving.

Conclusion:

Learning the art of weaving and carving in Vanuatu is an unforgettable journey into the cultural heritage of the islands. The hands-on experience, the wisdom shared by skilled artisans, and the profound cultural exchange make these workshops a transformative experience for travelers.

Through the art of weaving and carving, visitors can gain insights into the stories, beliefs, and traditions that have shaped Vanuatu's vibrant culture for generations. By supporting local artisans and embracing the craftsmanship of these ancient crafts, travelers play a crucial role in preserving Vanuatu's cultural heritage for future generations to cherish and celebrate.

So, immerse yourself in the world of weaving and carving, and discover the profound beauty of Vanuatu's cultural tapestry, one thread and one chisel stroke at a time.

Practical Tips for a Seamless Journey

Transportation within Vanuatu: Taxis, Buses, and Ferries

Vanuatu, a tropical paradise in the South Pacific, offers travelers an enchanting blend of natural beauty, vibrant culture, and warm hospitality. As you explore the archipelago's diverse islands, an important aspect of your journey is transportation. Understanding the transportation options within Vanuatu allows you to navigate between islands, explore remote destinations, and immerse yourself in the local way of life. In this comprehensive guide, we offer insider insights into the various transportation modes available, including taxis, buses, and ferries, to help you make the most of your travels in Vanuatu.

Taxis in Vanuatu: Convenience and Flexibility

Taxis are a popular mode of transportation for both locals and tourists in Vanuatu. In the main cities and tourist areas like Port Vila and Luganville, taxis are readily available and offer a convenient way to get around.

Taxis in Vanuatu are typically small minivans, known as "buses" by the locals. They are easy to spot with their red B sign on the front and back. Taxis are generally not metered, so it's important to agree on the fare with the driver before starting the journey. Negotiating the fare is common practice, and it's advisable to have small denominations of Vatu, the local currency, to pay the driver.

- Insider Tip: Taxis can be shared with other passengers, which is a cost-effective option. If you're comfortable with sharing the ride, let the driver know, and they will pick up additional passengers along the route.

Buses in Vanuatu: Experiencing Local Life

Buses, known as "bush buses," offer a more immersive and budget-friendly way to travel within Vanuatu. These brightly painted vehicles are a common sight on the islands and are a popular mode of transportation for locals going about their daily activities.

Bush buses follow set routes, connecting villages, towns, and various attractions. They provide an opportunity to interact with locals and experience the daily life and culture of the Ni-Vanuatu people. Buses can be a bit crowded, but they offer an authentic and memorable travel experience.

- Insider Tip: Buses may not have specific schedules, and they often depart when they are full. If you're on a tight schedule, it's best to plan your day accordingly and allow for some flexibility.

Rental Cars and Motorbikes: Exploring at Your Own Pace

For travelers who prefer the freedom to explore at their own pace, renting a car or motorbike is a popular option. Rental agencies are available in major cities and tourist hubs, offering a range of vehicles to suit different needs and budgets.

Renting a car or motorbike allows you to venture off the beaten path, explore remote areas, and access hidden gems that may not be easily reached by public transportation. It's a great way to take in the scenic beauty of the islands and embark on your adventures at your leisure.

- Insider Tip: Driving in Vanuatu follows the British system, with cars driving on the left side of the road. If you choose to rent a vehicle, familiarize yourself with local traffic rules and road conditions.

Inter-Island Ferries: Island Hopping Adventures

With Vanuatu being an archipelago of over 80 islands, inter-island ferries are essential for connecting different destinations. Ferries provide an opportunity for travelers to embark on exciting island hopping adventures and discover the unique charms of each island.

Ferries operate between the major islands like Efate, Espiritu Santo, Tanna, and Malakula, offering both passenger and cargo services. The ferries are equipped with basic amenities, and the journey itself can be a picturesque experience, with stunning views of the surrounding ocean and landscapes.

- Insider Tip: Ferry schedules may be subject to change due to weather conditions or other factors, so it's advisable to check the schedules in advance and be prepared for potential delays.

Domestic Flights: Fast and Convenient Island Connections

For travelers looking to cover longer distances between islands quickly, domestic flights are available from the main airports in Port Vila and Luganville. Domestic airlines like Air Vanuatu and Unity Airlines operate regular flights to several destinations across Vanuatu.

Domestic flights are particularly convenient for reaching more remote or less accessible islands, such as those in the Torba and Penama provinces. The aerial views of Vanuatu's stunning landscapes and turquoise waters are a bonus during these short flights.

- Insider Tip: Domestic flights can book up quickly, especially during peak tourist seasons. It's advisable to book your flights in advance to secure your preferred travel dates.

Safety Considerations for Transportation:

- Sea Travel: When traveling by boat or ferry, be mindful of sea conditions, especially during the cyclone season (November to April). If you're prone to seasickness, consider taking medication or opting for a domestic flight instead.
- Road Conditions: Some roads on the islands may be unpaved or in rough condition, especially in more rural areas. Exercise caution and drive carefully, particularly if you're renting a car or motorbike.
- Local Knowledge: Engage with local drivers, guides, and transportation providers for valuable insights into the best routes, scenic spots, and cultural experiences during your travels.

Conclusion:

Understanding the transportation options within Vanuatu is essential for making the most of your journey through this tropical paradise. From taxis and buses for a more immersive experience to rental cars and domestic flights for flexibility and convenience, each mode of transportation offers unique insights into the cultural richness and natural beauty of the islands.

By choosing sustainable and responsible transportation options, supporting local businesses, and engaging with the Ni-Vanuatu people, travelers can create a positive impact and contribute to the preservation of Vanuatu's unique heritage. Embrace the adventure of island hopping, immerse yourself in local life, and explore the breathtaking landscapes that Vanuatu has to offer. Let the spirit of the islands guide your journey as you navigate through the azure waters and lush landscapes, creating lasting memories of your time in this enchanting South Pacific destination.

Language and Communication

Vanuatu, with its diverse cultures and languages, presents an exciting linguistic landscape for travelers seeking to connect with the local communities and immerse themselves in the cultural tapestry of the islands. Communication is a powerful tool that fosters understanding and meaningful connections. In this comprehensive guide, we explore the languages spoken in Vanuatu, offer insights into the importance of language in Ni-Vanuatu culture, and provide useful phrases to help travelers communicate with locals during their stay.

Linguistic Diversity in Vanuatu:

Vanuatu is home to an astonishing linguistic diversity, with over 110 languages spoken across the archipelago. This remarkable diversity is a testament to the distinct cultural identities of the different communities that call the islands home.

The three official languages of Vanuatu are Bislama, English, and French. Bislama, a creole language, serves as a lingua franca and is widely understood and spoken by most Ni-Vanuatu people. English and French are used for official and administrative purposes, but their usage is more limited in everyday communication.

- Insider Tip: While English and French are not commonly used in daily interactions, learning a few basic phrases in Bislama can go a long way in connecting with locals and showing appreciation for their culture.

The Significance of Language in Ni-Vanuatu Culture:

Language holds deep cultural significance in Ni-Vanuatu culture. Each language reflects the history, customs, and unique way of life of the communities that speak it. Language is not just a means of communication; it is an integral part of identity and plays a vital role in preserving cultural heritage.

For the Ni-Vanuatu people, using their native language is a way of expressing pride in their cultural roots and passing down traditional knowledge from one generation to another. It is a source of unity and strength that binds communities together.

- Insider Tip: When interacting with locals, showing interest in their language and culture is a gesture of respect and appreciation that is warmly received.

Useful Phrases in Bislama:

Bislama, also known as Bichelama or Bislam, is a unique creole language that developed as a means of communication between diverse language groups in Vanuatu. It is a simplified form of English, with influences from local languages and French. Learning a few phrases in Bislama will not only help you communicate with locals but also enrich your cultural experience.

Hello: Halo or Halo yu

Thank you: Tangkyu tumas

Yes: Yes or Ya

No: No or Nomo

How are you?: Yu stap gut?

I'm fine: Mi stap gut

What is your name?: Wanem nem blong yu?

My name is...: Nem blong mi...

Goodbye: Gudbai

Please: Plis

Excuse me / Sorry: Sori

Help: Helpim mi

I don't understand: Mi no save

Where is...?: We i stap...?

How much is this?: Hem ia hemi costem?

- Insider Tip: Ni-Vanuatu people are appreciative of visitors who make an effort to speak Bislama. Don't be shy to use these phrases during your interactions—it will be warmly received.

Non-Verbal Communication:

In addition to spoken language, non-verbal communication also plays a significant role in Ni-Vanuatu culture. Handshakes, smiles, and nods are common forms of greeting and showing respect. Paying attention to cultural cues and body language can help facilitate better understanding and connection during your interactions.

- Insider Tip: In some cultures within Vanuatu, eye contact may be seen as disrespectful or aggressive. Be observant of local customs and adapt your behavior accordingly.

Embracing Cultural Differences:

As a culturally diverse country, Vanuatu celebrates and embraces its many languages and traditions.

Travelers can enhance their experience by showing curiosity and openness to the diverse customs and ways of life they encounter.

Language barriers may exist, but they also present an opportunity for learning, discovery, and cross-cultural exchange. A smile and a willingness to engage can bridge gaps and create meaningful connections with the people you meet.

- Insider Tip: Locals are often eager to share their culture and traditions with curious travelers. Be open to learning from them and appreciate the unique perspectives they offer.

Conclusion:

Language and communication are the keys to unlocking the cultural richness and diversity of Vanuatu. Embracing the local languages, particularly Bislama, opens doors to authentic experiences and meaningful connections with the Ni-Vanuatu people.

By using a few simple phrases in Bislama and being attentive to non-verbal cues, travelers can navigate the linguistic landscape of Vanuatu with respect and ease. Embrace the cultural differences, show curiosity, and be open to learning from the communities you encounter. In doing so, you'll not only enrich your own travel experience but also create lasting memories of the warm and welcoming spirit of Vanuatu and its treasured people.

Health and Safety Guidelines

Vanuatu, with its stunning landscapes and vibrant culture, is a dream destination for many travelers seeking a tropical paradise. As you embark on your journey to this South Pacific archipelago, it is essential to prioritize your health and safety to ensure a memorable and worry-free experience. In this comprehensive guide, we provide essential health and safety guidelines for travelers in Vanuatu, covering everything from vaccinations and health precautions to water safety and cultural considerations.

Vaccinations and Health Precautions:

Before traveling to Vanuatu, it is recommended to consult with a travel health specialist or your healthcare provider to ensure you are up-to-date with routine vaccinations and receive any additional vaccinations required for the region.

The following vaccinations are typically recommended for travelers to Vanuatu:

- Routine vaccinations (e.g., measles, mumps, rubella, tetanus, diphtheria, and pertussis)
- Hepatitis A and B
- Typhoid
- Yellow fever (for travelers coming from yellow fever risk countries)

Malaria is present in Vanuatu, so it's important to take malaria prophylaxis medication as prescribed and use mosquito repellent, long-sleeved clothing, and mosquito nets while sleeping to minimize the risk of mosquito-borne diseases.

Insider Tip: Carry a basic first aid kit with essential medications, bandages, and antiseptics for minor injuries and illnesses.

Hygiene and Food Safety:

Maintaining good hygiene practices is crucial to avoid food and waterborne illnesses. Follow these tips to stay healthy during your travels in Vanuatu:

Drink only bottled water or boiled and filtered water.

- Avoid consuming raw or undercooked food, as well as street food from unhygienic vendors.
- Wash your hands frequently with soap and water, especially before eating.
- Insider Tip: Fresh fruit and coconut water are delicious treats in Vanuatu, but ensure they are thoroughly washed or peeled before consumption.

Sun Protection:

With its tropical climate, Vanuatu experiences high temperatures and intense sun. Protect yourself from sunburn and heat-related illnesses by:

- Wearing wide-brimmed hats, sunglasses, and light, loose-fitting clothing.

- Applying sunscreen with a high SPF regularly, especially if engaging in water activities.
- Staying hydrated by drinking plenty of water throughout the day.
- Insider Tip: Seek shade during the hottest hours of the day, typically between 10 AM and 3 PM, to avoid direct exposure to the sun.

Water Safety:

Vanuatu's pristine waters are inviting, but it's important to exercise caution and follow water safety guidelines:

- Swim only in designated swimming areas and heed any warning signs.
- Pay attention to local advice regarding rip currents and other potential hazards.
- When snorkeling or diving, use reputable operators with experienced guides and follow their safety protocols.
- Insider Tip: Check the tide and weather conditions before going swimming or participating in water activities.

Respect Local Customs and Traditions:

Vanuatu has a rich cultural heritage, and it's essential to show respect for local customs and traditions. Some key cultural considerations include:

- Dress modestly, especially when visiting villages or attending ceremonies.
- Always ask for permission before taking photos of people or their property.
- Avoid pointing with your finger, as it can be considered impolite in some cultures.
- Insider Tip: Engaging with locals in a friendly and respectful manner can lead to meaningful cultural exchanges and enrich your travel experience.

Insect Bites and Mosquito Protection:

- Protecting yourself from insect bites is vital in Vanuatu to avoid diseases such as dengue fever and Zika virus. Follow these tips:
- Use insect repellent containing DEET on exposed skin and clothing.
- Sleep under mosquito nets, especially in open-air accommodations.
- Insider Tip: Wear light-colored, long-sleeved shirts and long pants to reduce the likelihood of mosquito bites.

Conclusion:

Prioritizing your health and safety during your travels in Vanuatu is essential for a smooth and enjoyable experience. By following these health and safety guidelines, you can explore the natural beauty, immerse yourself in the rich cultural heritage, and create unforgettable memories in this tropical paradise. Remember to prepare in advance, stay informed, and take necessary precautions to protect yourself and fully embrace the wonders of Vanuatu with peace of mind.

Vanuatu itineraries

One week itineraries

Vanuatu, with its breathtaking landscapes and vibrant culture, offers a myriad of experiences for travelers to indulge in. Whether you're seeking adventure, relaxation, or cultural immersion, the islands have something to offer. Below are two detailed one-week itineraries to help you make the most of your time in Vanuatu.

Itinerary 1: Adventure and Nature Exploration

Day 1: Arrival in Port Vila, Efate Island

- Arrive in Port Vila, the capital of Vanuatu, and settle into your accommodation.
- Explore the local markets, sample fresh tropical fruits, and purchase handicrafts as souvenirs.
- Visit the Port Vila Waterfront and enjoy a relaxing evening overlooking the ocean.

Day 2: Mele Cascades and Blue Lagoon, Efate Island

- Embark on a morning excursion to Mele Cascades, a beautiful waterfall surrounded by lush rainforest.
- Take a refreshing dip in the natural pools and hike to the top for breathtaking views.

- In the afternoon, head to the Blue Lagoon, a stunning freshwater swimming hole perfect for snorkeling and relaxation.

Day 3: Tanna Island and Mount Yasur Volcano

- Take a short domestic flight to Tanna Island.
- Visit the fascinating Yakel Village to learn about traditional customs and village life.
- In the evening, experience the awe-inspiring Mount Yasur Volcano, one of the world's most accessible active volcanoes. Witness the fiery glow as it erupts against the night sky.

Day 4: Tanna Island and Cultural Immersion

- Spend the morning exploring more of Tanna's cultural villages and interacting with friendly locals.
- Visit the stunning White Grass Ocean Resort & Spa for a relaxing afternoon on the beach.

Day 5: Espiritu Santo Island: Blue Holes and Champagne Beach

Fly to Espiritu Santo Island, known for its pristine beaches and underwater wonders.

- Discover the mystical Blue Holes, a network of crystal-clear freshwater swimming spots amidst lush jungle.

- Relax on Champagne Beach, famous for its sparkling turquoise waters and powdery white sand.

Day 6: Espiritu Santo Island: Lonnoc Beach and SS President Coolidge

- Visit Lonnoc Beach, a picturesque destination framed by limestone cliffs and natural rock pools.
- Dive the SS President Coolidge, a World War II wreck teeming with marine life and history.

Day 7: Return to Port Vila and Departure

- Fly back to Port Vila, Efate Island.
- Spend your last day at leisure, exploring any missed spots or relaxing on the beach.
- Depart from Vanuatu with unforgettable memories of your adventure-filled week.

Itinerary 2: Cultural Immersion and Relaxation

Day 1: Arrival in Port Vila, Efate Island

- Arrive in Port Vila and check into your accommodation.
- Stroll along the picturesque seafront and explore the vibrant town center.
- Sample local delicacies at a traditional Melanesian feast for dinner.

Day 2: Cultural Tours in Efate Island

- Begin your cultural immersion with a visit to Ekasup Cultural Village to learn about traditional practices and customs.
- Explore the National Museum of Vanuatu to gain insights into the country's rich history and cultural diversity.

Day 3: Tranquility at Hideaway Island, Efate Island

- Take a boat to Hideaway Island, renowned for its crystal-clear waters and underwater post office.
- Enjoy snorkeling, diving, or simply lounging on the secluded beach.

Day 4: Tanna Island: Custom and Village Life

- Fly to Tanna Island and experience local customs at Imaio Village.
- Participate in traditional dance performances and interact with the welcoming community.

Day 5: Tanna Island: Yasur Volcano and Relaxation

- Witness the powerful eruptions of Mount Yasur Volcano at sunrise or sunset.
- Spend the afternoon unwinding at a serene beachfront resort.

Day 6: Return to Port Vila and Iririki Island Retreat

- Return to Port Vila and take a short boat ride to Iririki Island.
- Indulge in luxury and relaxation at a private island resort.

Day 7: Departure from Port Vila

Enjoy your final day at Iririki Island, with the option of spa treatments or water activities.

Depart from Vanuatu with cherished memories of the cultural experiences and tranquil moments.

Conclusion:

Whether you choose an adventurous itinerary filled with nature exploration or a cultural immersion and relaxation journey, Vanuatu promises an unforgettable experience. Customize your one-week itinerary based on your interests, and be sure to embrace the warm hospitality and vibrant culture of the Ni-Vanuatu people. Whichever path you take, Vanuatu's beauty and charm will leave you with lasting memories and a desire to return to this enchanting paradise.

Weekend itineraries

Vanuatu, with its stunning natural beauty, vibrant culture, and warm hospitality, offers a plethora of experiences for travelers seeking an unforgettable adventure in the South Pacific. In these detailed week-long itineraries, we provide two different options that showcase the best of Vanuatu, including island hopping, water activities, cultural immersion, and relaxation. Whether you're an adventurous explorer or a culture enthusiast, these itineraries cater to different interests and ensure a well-rounded and memorable experience.

Option 1: Island Hopping and Adventure Extravaganza

Day 1: Arrive in Port Vila, Efate

- Explore Port Vila's vibrant markets and waterfront area.
- Visit the Vanuatu Cultural Centre to gain insights into the country's rich cultural heritage.
- Enjoy a sunset cruise to set the tone for a magical week ahead.

Day 2: Mele Cascades and Blue Lagoon, Efate

- Take a refreshing morning dip at the Mele Cascades waterfall and enjoy a guided hike through lush rainforest.
- Spend the afternoon at the stunning Blue Lagoon, where you can swim in crystal-clear waters and try out some water sports activities.

Day 3: Hideaway Island and Snorkeling, Efate

- Embark on a short boat ride to Hideaway Island, a snorkeler's paradise.
- Explore the underwater post office and swim with colorful marine life.

Day 4: Espiritu Santo Island

- Take a domestic flight to Espiritu Santo Island, known for its natural beauty and pristine beaches.
- Relax on Champagne Beach, one of the most beautiful beaches in the world.

Day 5: Millenium Cave Tour, Espiritu Santo Island

- Embark on a thrilling adventure through the Millenium Cave, a stunning underground river cave.
- Swim, jump, and float your way through the cave and witness its breathtaking beauty.

Day 6: Pentecost Island (Land Diving Season Only)

- During land diving season (April to June), take a short flight to Pentecost Island.
- Witness the famous land diving ritual, where local men jump from tall wooden towers with

vines tied to their ankles, symbolizing a bountiful yam harvest.

Day 7: Back to Efate, Departure

- Return to Efate and spend your last day relaxing on the beach or exploring Port Vila's local attractions.
- Depart with cherished memories of Vanuatu's adventure-filled week.

Option 2: Cultural Immersion and Relaxation Retreat

Day 1: Arrive in Port Vila, Efate

- Settle into your accommodation and take a leisurely walk along the picturesque Port Vila waterfront.
- Enjoy a relaxing evening by the beach and savor the local cuisine.

Day 2: Ekasup Cultural Village, Efate

- Immerse yourself in Vanuatu's traditional customs and way of life at the Ekasup Cultural Village.
- Participate in cultural activities, learn traditional dances, and enjoy a traditional feast.
- Day 3: Relaxation and Beach Time, Efate
- Spend the day at one of Efate's tranquil beaches, such as Eton Beach or Pango Beach.

- Indulge in a relaxing massage or spa treatment to unwind.

Day 4: Tanna Island

- Take a domestic flight to Tanna Island and experience the unique customs and traditions of the local communities.
- Visit the Yakel Village to witness ancient practices and interact with the people of Tanna.

Day 5: Mount Yasur Volcano, Tanna Island

- Embark on a guided trek to the rim of Mount Yasur, one of the most accessible active volcanoes in the world.
- Witness the mesmerizing lava lake and experience the awe-inspiring power of nature.

Day 6: Relaxation and Reflection, Efate

- Return to Efate for a day of relaxation and reflection.
- Take a sunset cruise to end the day on a peaceful note.

Day 7: Departure

- Spend your final morning exploring the local markets for souvenirs and gifts.
- Depart with a heart full of cultural experiences and fond memories of your week in Vanuatu.

Conclusion:

Vanuatu offers a diverse range of experiences for travelers seeking adventure, cultural immersion, and relaxation. These week-long itineraries cater to different interests and highlight the best that the archipelago has to offer. Whether you choose to embark on an island hopping extravaganza or embrace a cultural immersion and relaxation retreat, Vanuatu promises an unforgettable journey filled with warmth, wonder, and the spirit of the South Pacific

Conclusion

In conclusion, Vanuatu, the jewel of the South Pacific, beckons travelers with its breathtaking natural beauty, vibrant culture, and warm hospitality. From stunning beaches to lush jungles, active volcanoes to colorful festivals, this archipelago offers a diverse range of experiences for every adventurer.

As you immerse yourself in the melodic languages, explore cultural villages, and savor local delicacies, you'll find yourself embraced by the spirit of Vanuatu and its people. Whether you choose an action-packed adventure, a tranquil retreat, or a blend of both, this tropical paradise has something to offer every traveler.

As you journey through Vanuatu's islands, keep in mind the importance of responsible tourism. Respect for the environment, appreciation for cultural diversity, and support for local communities contribute to the preservation of this magical destination for future generations to enjoy.

So, embark on this extraordinary journey to Vanuatu and unlock the secrets of its enchanting landscapes, traditions, and warm-hearted people. The memories you create and the experiences you encounter will undoubtedly leave a lasting impression, forever etching Vanuatu in your heart as a place of wonder, joy, and discovery.

In the words of the Ni-Vanuatu people: "Tankyu tumas" (Thank you very much) for exploring this paradise with an open heart and adventurous spirit. We look forward to welcoming you to Vanuatu soon, where your dreams of a South Pacific paradise come true.

Made in United States
Orlando, FL
06 February 2024

43371158R00075